MEN: A FIELD GUIDE

by Peter Murdoch and Peter Maddocks

Aided and abetted by Emma Dawson

MEN
A FIELD GUIDE

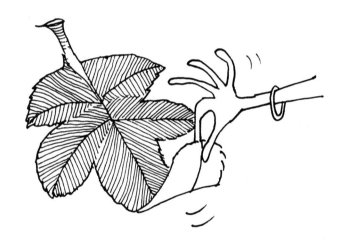

A New English Library Original Publication, 1983

First NEL Paperback Edition October 1983

NEL Books are published by
New English Library,
Mill Road, Dunton Green,
Sevenoaks, Kent.
Editorial office: 47 Bedford Square, London WC1B 3DP

Made and printed in Great Britain by
Fletcher & Son Ltd, Norwich
0 450 05622 8

Maddocks, Peter
Men.
1. Men – Anecdotes, facetiae, satire, etc.
2. Women – Anecdotes, facetiae, satire, etc.
3. Sex role – Anecdotes, facetiae, satire, etc.
4. Interpersonal relations – Anecdotes, facetiae, satire, etc.
I. Title   II. Murdoch, Peter
III. Dawson, Emma
305.3'0207   HM132
ISBN 0 450 05622 8

Contents

Page

AUTHORS' FOREWORD   **9**

HOW TO USE THIS BOOK   **11**

HAS MAN REALLY PROGRESSED?   **12**

ONCE A MAN, TWICE A BOY   **14**

WHAT MAKES A MAN TICK?   **16**

THE FUNDAMENTALS covering: **18**
Education and Background, Character and Mood,
Mother Influence, Intellect, Virility, Givers and
Takers, Presentation, Build, Collectors and
Non-Collectors.

HOW TO SCORE   **56**

THE CHARACTERS – 28 standard examples, interspersed with comments on: **59**
sleeping habits; nasty habits; disgusting habits;
bathroom habits; risk takers; influence of
alcohol; the single man; the married man; sexual
fantasies; sexual variations and deviations;
exercise freaks; the emotional man; eating
habits; foreigners

SO WHAT'S THE SCORE? – The Experts' Score Charts   **155**

THE MANALYSIS CHART – Your Chance to Score Your Man   **158**

*Every character
in this book bears
every
resemblance to
everyone we've
ever met.*

Equality - is it worth it?

Foreword

We offer this book to all womankind as a comprehensive guide to recognizing and understanding Men. It is written by two men, who just wish women would understand them better, and by one woman - who perhaps knows no better.

It is our contribution towards helping men and women live together in a better harmony; through indicating how to make the right choice for you in the first place; and thereafter to lead you to a greater understanding of why your man does the things he does where and when he does them so that they don't take you by surprise, so that you can make room to accommodate them, and even - where appropriate - so that you can help him overcome some of his more unfortunate dispositions.

It is the product of long, intensive, loving - and even reckless - research. Behind this book is much lurking in alleyways, behatted and darkly clothed; clambering up drainpipes, periscope in hand; drowning in deluges, gum-booted and photo-lensed; inserting spyholes in bathroom doors; secreting microphones in bedrooms and loos; clinging to the guttering and dangling miniature tape-recorders outside windows; drinking too much in pubs and wine-bars; rushing film to the labs at midnight for secret processing; getting arrested for suspected homosexual loitering, or plain soliciting, outside men's clubs; and watching, watching, watching.

All to bring to you the broadest range of men in all their aspects that we possibly could. All to unearth for you those most peculiar and secret of men's emotions and habits. All to help you learn how to spot the right man for you and, having spotted him, how to disentangle all those confusing component parts, understand what they each mean, and how they all interrelate and function together in that mysterious, often seemingly contradictory amalgam called MAN.

How to use this book

Fundamentally, this book is to be *used;* to be read, taken into the field, practised on, analyised and put into effect. It's a book of How to Identify Men, and also How to Keep Them in Captivity, Health and Happiness. And you, too.

It deals with all common - and not-so-common - species of men who surround us in our daily lives. Some migrant species are included. No extinct species are covered.

It analyses both their physiological and psychological aspects; their plumage; their behavioural characteristics; their habitats; breeding habits; domestic habits; social habits; anti-social habits; external influences; survival rating; occupations and pre-occupations; feeding habits; drinking habits; gambits and ruses; fantasies, hopes and fears; community activities; sequential and consequential attitudes; and then more habits.

It is an attempt to help you identify the various sorts of men and, having identified them, what to do about it and how to understand them - if that is what you want to do about it.

Once you have acquired the basic formula, no special skills are required for spotting. Deeper and more precise analysis obviously demannds a greater familiarity of the man concerned, but certainly normal social intercourse following the guidance of this book will help you to assess whether you wish to attain that deeper analysis.

Spotting can be done anywhere and at any time that there are men around. Pubs, wine bars and clubs are obviously natural hunting grounds, but the domestic environment is important and even general observations in the streets or on public transport can be enlightening.

For the general spotter, no specialist equipment is required apart from this book, a pencil and maybe a note pad. For those who wish to become experts, concealed microphones and closed-circuit televisions are useful tools, and plenty of trial and error through practise. This book will help you; don't ever lose it - or if you do, buy another one. Immediately.

Has man really progressed?

Nature has actually been rather unkind to man. And it's probably more due to the dependence of woman during pregnancy and then of both woman and child during the long up-bringing than anything else. When a man would really like to be out hunting, fighting and generally playing the field, he remembers - fortunately - his innate sense of responsibility for and pride in his family. So Man had to become Civilised and evolve all sorts of complex social structures, which really he views as social strictures.

When it was all still rather primitive and something of a game, and Life was fundamentally simple, he probably quite enjoyed the Little Woman being dependent on him, looking after him, adoring and admiring him and, most important, belonging to him. But the progression of our so-called civilisation hasn't allowed it all to

remain so free and basic. He's had to learn how to be subtle, cunning and even devious, but it doesn't really come naturally.

So all that Sophistication is very much a veneer. The Basic is strong in man, and to understand him better you must never overlook that cardinal fact. More intelligent men will use their minds to overcome as much as possible the Matter - but the Matter is always there. Don't forget that - and beware of expecting your man to be what you think the Modern Sophisticated Man should be. That expectation is at a far remove from reality and is one of society's major distorting factors and at the root of many a divorce or nervous breakdown.

Accept Him for What He Is. Don't drive him to drink.

Once a man, twice a boy

Everybody knows that men reach their physical peak very young. What is less often discussed is man's mental peak, which he should reach around middle age - the mid-life crisis often marked by the taking of a young mistress, a change in the clothes he wears, and Keeping Fit. Some will grow beards and sail around the world.

From here on, it's the long, slow decline; the short-term memory starts to decay, and memories of the Good Old Days start flooding back with a vengeance. The days when they were All Boys Together - and you can expect heightened interest in sport to develop, along with more regular reunions and sessions in the pub or club. Extreme cases will revert back to nappy changes and short trousers.

It's rotten for them, if you think about it. Families to support, careers to be taken seriously, people all around them who need impressing, maybe mistresses to be kept enthralled. When all they really want to do is curl up with a can of beer in front of the afternoon's football and be thoroughly looked-after.

Make your man *feel* properly cherished and nurtured - even if you can only manage it sporadically - and he'll love you and look after *you* for ever. Remember - all men need to feel Mothered.

What makes a man tick?

Anyone who's ever been to classes in car maintenance will know that the only way to maintain a car in peak condition so that it will operate smoothly for you and do what you ask it to do is to understand the workings of and limitations to that car's engine.

It's remarkably similar with men. Once you've got to grips with the salient and fundamental characteristics that are common to all men, individual character analysis is a relatively straight-forward business.

Nine characteristics have been isolated and explored in the following sections as being of primary importance in explaining a man's actions, motivations and feelings. Obviously there are more, and obviously generalisation is the order of the day, since the variations are as numerous as there are men. But the basis is sound and comprehensive.

Some of these fundamentals are a product of heredity and upbringing; others a function of physical and mental attributes (or lack of them); some are just personal and individual character traits. None can be taken in isolation except for the purpose of deep character analysis and rating, and all are common to all men.

Once you have read and digested the funda-mentals, it is to be hoped that you will never again assess a man with any preconceived ideas of what he should and shouldn't be like. Nor will you automatically *expect* a man to behave in the way *you* think he should. What you think and what he thinks are liable to be poles apart until you have really taken the trouble to get to the root of it all.

The roots start with the fundamentals. Get digging.

You will notice that a scoring system is included. For a full explanation, see 'How to Score' (p. 56). It's the absolute basis of successful man-spotting.

EDUCATION (a jaundiced view)

Trained to become groupies. Organisation and family-business men. Where there are men yahooing and braying and boozing, there are the Old Boys. Don't really understand women, and don't particularly want to. Extreme cases can veer towards homosexuality. Drink (Scotch on the Rocks) to overcome basic social awkwardness. Talk loudly and laugh at their own jokes. Know exactly how to Put the World to Rights. Women have their uses - washing socks, lying on their backs thinking of . . . . . - then it's off to the club/race course/political meeting. Will prosper because they already have money, and know how to play the game. If you want a lonely, secure, submissive life, they aren't hard to spot.

Rating: UNATTRACTIVE IN PARTS 4

If they manage to overcome the disadvantaged start, they will succeed, and succeed well. Can be too aggressive and pushy - ever-hungry. Wind up on the Nouveau Riche status-symbol kick. Never satisfied; bossy, angry, lonely and emotionally vacillating. Don't really belong anywhere, and try extra hard to be nice and to impress. Often take dolly-bird mistresses whom they shower with extravagant goodies. Wife is put up as a front. You'd get a good divorce settlement.

Rating: UNFORTUNATE 2

If they accept their lot, and do their best, you have the solid, honest, dependable back-bone of society. Terrific family men. Will work doubly hard to send their children to private education. Will never make for a champagne-swilling, Bahama-cruising life, but to be taken seriously.

Rating: SOUND 8

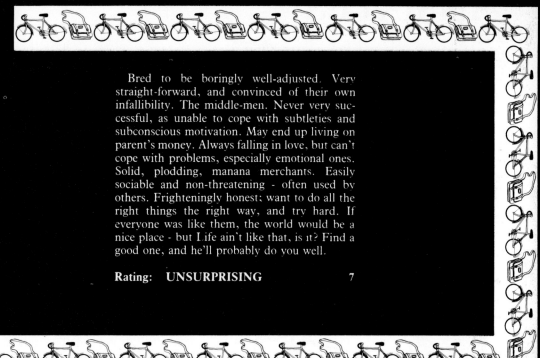

Bred to be boringly well-adjusted. Very straight-forward, and convinced of their own infallibility. The middle-men. Never very successful, as unable to cope with subtleties and subconscious motivation. May end up living on parent's money. Always falling in love, but can't cope with problems, especially emotional ones. Solid, plodding, manana merchants. Easily sociable and non-threatening - often used by others. Frighteningly honest; want to do all the right things the right way, and try hard. If everyone was like them, the world would be a nice place - but Life ain't like that, is it? Find a good one, and he'll probably do you well.

Rating: UNSURPRISING   7

UNDER GRAD

Trained to believe they're special and better. If they are - fine; the country needs them and, if they have a streak of humility and charity also, you can rate them highly - although you'll always play second-fiddle to their latest invention or philosophical treatise.

Rating: CREDIBLE   8

But watch out for those who don't make it; the Undergrad Rats, cornered by failure. Beneath a polished veneer of suave wheeling and dealing in a fantasy world is a sour, vicious, bitter and dishonest con-man. Poseurs; elitist and trendy, forever popping corks with a flourish and talking about The Big Deal just around the corner. No time to do an honest day's work, or think of anyone but themselves.

Rating: AVOID LIKE THE PLAGUE   0

INMATES

The beginnings are basic. Your man kicked off as a kid – and his early schoolboy pack life will have taken its toll. If you can find out – by fair means or foul – what he was like as a boy, you've set the scene for what he is today. Start sneaking into the old family photo albums.

The Undergrad:

Has spent longer cocooned in the environment of institutional education and the parental home. Creamed off as prime induction material – groomed for leadership. Postpones the assumption of adult responsibility – but has longer to find his real niche. If successful, likely to be more interesting and well-balanced than other men. Most leaders come from this group – whether anarchic or conformist.

The Swot:

The etiolated weed. Enjoys learning. Ostracised by his peers, so may grow up rather lonely. Much fraternising with adults as a child. Shy and sensitive – or hyper self-confident. Thoughtful. Could be frail.

The Bully-Boy:

Soon learns his only strength *is* his strength. Can only progress by bashing everyone else out of the way. Fear is his Key. Sadistic. Thick, dull, ineffectual and thoroughly unpleasant. Unkempt. Picks his nose with dirty fingernails. Snarls. To be found building railways, or behind bars.

The Tearaway:
Standard gang material. Practical joker and arsonist. Knows all the dirty tricks. Won't learn. Could grow up to be great fun, if totally irresponsible. Accident-prone. Very active – well developed physically. Leader material. Likely to live long – unless knocked down by a bus.

Billy Bunter:
Mummy's little boy – always being fed up. Assumes role of fun-figure in the pack, which some grow to like and need: their only way of being Special. Lack of athleticism. Can be sad and insecure – food is The Comforter. Could be hormonal defect. Heavy on the housekeeping – quite apart from anything else.

Teacher's Pet:
Usually *loathed* by all other boys. Gets promoted into all roles of seniority and responsibility – whether capable or not. A natural acolyte. Knows who to impress, and how. The undiscerning sycophant. Wallows in his own glory. Could have sadistic tendencies.

CHARACTER

C

S

P

M

Mr Choleric

All over the place. The yo-yo. Healthily ambivalent, but can tend to extremes. Know the heights and depths and understand them. Sensitive and thoughtful. Caring, creative. All the exciting great men come from this category. Talented and intelligent; alert; all-rounder; both gregarious and needful of solitude. The most complex and interesting; generally fun to be with. Excellent in bed - on a good day. Can be unpredictable.

Rating: FASCINATING   10

Mr Melancholic

The Below-the-Liner. Buried in volcanic ashes; doom and gloom; it's always raining; it's always Monday morning. Humourless. Read 'The Telegraph'; carry chips on both shoulders. Always complaining - especially at everyone else's inadequacies. Uncreative, unimaginative; dull in very respect - including sexually. Boorish; want to be waited on hand and foot. Tend to be bossy. Probably faithful - get settled into a rut of complaining and feel safe there. Possibly Celtic. Worry about worrying. Will die young.

Rating: FOR MASOCHISTS   0

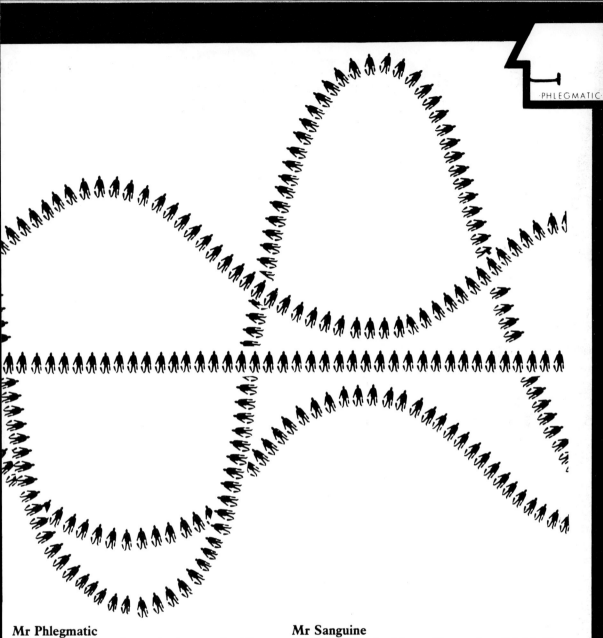

Mr Phlegmatic

He *is* The Line. Pretty boring, really. If you want secuity, here's your man. Non-creative, methodologist - do everything by the rule book. Plodding; a little pernickety. Mr. Average Family Man. Uninspired and uninspiring; don't naturally shine at anything, but can succeed through obduracy. Well-dressed, but conventionally and anonymously. Thorougly Nice and Normal. Play sport once a week or jog. Propose on one knee and remember anniversaries.

Rating: PLAUSIBLE   6

Mr Sanguine

The Above-the-Liner. Always cheerful; bluff, hale and hearty. Devil-may-care. Never worry (so they think). Totally insensitive. Make very good businessmen and disastrous bull-in-a-china-shop lovers. Very presumptous; noisy and showy; loud talkers and dressers. Tend to make other men feel inferior; aggressive; self-publicist, arrogant; rather brash and uncaring. Suffer from allergies.

Rating: TIRESOME   2

SAN

CHARACTERS

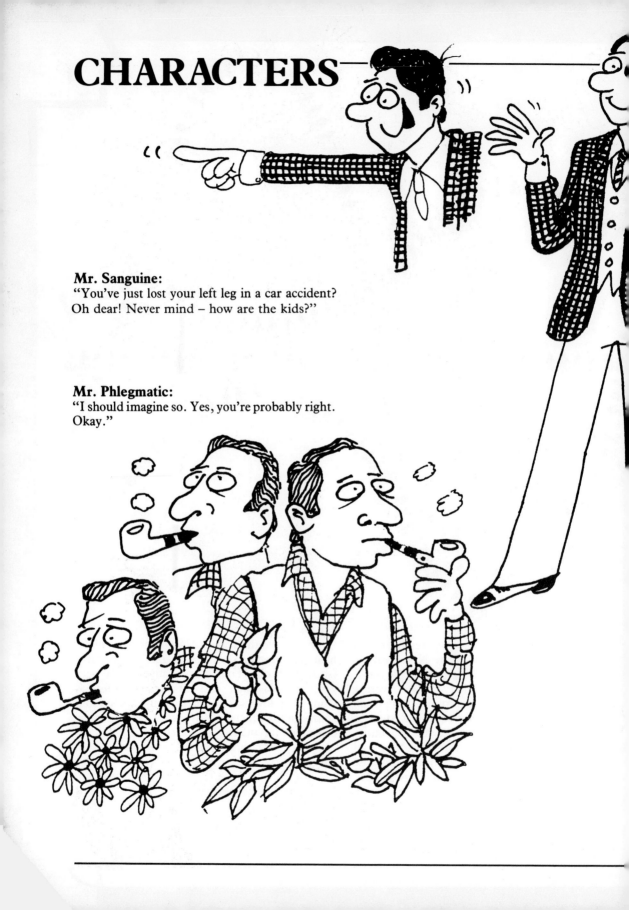

Mr. Sanguine:
"You've just lost your left leg in a car accident?
Oh dear! Never mind – how are the kids?"

Mr. Phlegmatic:
"I should imagine so. Yes, you're probably right.
Okay."

Choleric:
t of course! How marvellous . . . *You said*
? HOW DARE YOU!!"

Melancholic:
d you so, didn't I?"

MOTHERS

All men are Mother-dominated to some degree. A thought that has doubtless occurred to you - but do you realise just how important that degree of mother-influence actually is?

Mother reincarnate

Definitely and totally Mum-dominated. Probably from single-parent family, no Dad. Need a mother-surrogate. Normal ladies are too like Mum for comfort, so consequently tend to go for tarty ladies, and lots of them. Find relationships with women difficult, and women slightly threatening. Might even veer to homosexuality. Likes nightclubs, flash cars and jewellery. Slightly narcissistic - wash a lot - usually smell pretty.

Rating: AVOID   **0**

Mum's Son

Largely Mum-dominated. Probably from Matriarchal family with subservient Dad. Similar to Mother reincarnate types, but less extravagantly so. Often very aggressive and successful in business, but need to be dominated at home. Will don an apron and help around the house; very family-loving, but will probably sneak off for a quick one on the side. Can't cook.

Rating: MALLEABLE   **2**

Sorry Mum?

Dad away from home a lot, so Mum figures importantly through circumstance rather than personality. Bachelor types. Read dirty magazines and like well-endowed tarty ladies with peroxide hair. Slightly insecure; pleasure seeking; identity seeking. Love being surrounded by groups of people. Rather hard to pin down.

Rating: NEBULOUS   **5**

Yes-Mum

Normal family background, but tougher than average Mum - possibly a business woman. Fairly straightforward; normal sexual relationships; probably faithful; quite trainable; could be slightly effeminate, sometimes. Rather a loner, but need groups and security. Love women, but probably don't like them very much. Can usually cook and mend their own clothes.

Rating: REASONABLE   **7**

Okay Mum

Equal influence of Mum and Dad, or stronger than average paternal influence. Rather shy, but popular, easy-going and confident. Capable and probably successful. Few sexual hang-ups. Tend to be quite dominant without being aggressive - not-too-fussed. Slightly selfish. Basically faithful, but attractive to other women, so beware. Good in the garden, but lousy around the house.

Rating: PREFERABLE   **10**

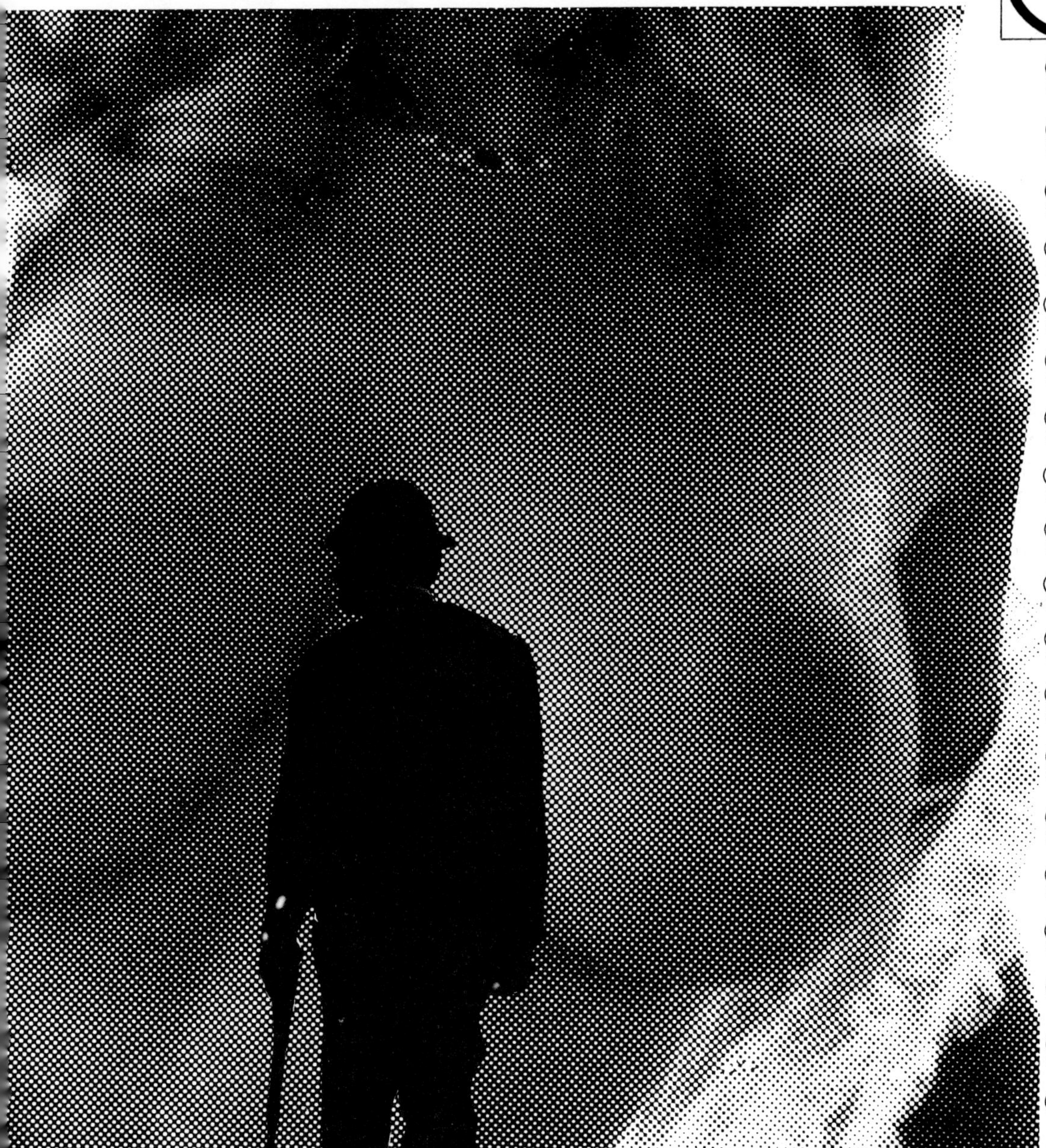

MOTHERS

Definitely a tricky area, and to be handled with as much caution and perspicacity as you can muster. Whilst all Mums are different, there are some cardinal factors that remain constant. To all Mums, their sons are their Little Darlings who never really grow up, and no girl can possibly be quite good enough for Their Boy. Mother-and-Son combinations can be formidable in the extreme, especially if mum and son are very alike. Watch her closely - her son is usually going to expect the same of you - particularly the very Mum-dominated types. On your first visit to the Family Home, take a note pad and jot down salient facts - cooking? domestic? intellectual? trendy? Take note of the sort of presents they give you - are they hinting at something? Take care how you analyse what your man says to you about his mum. He may be derogatory about her from time to time, but essentially she can do no wrong in his eyes, and you can *never* be derogatory about her.

Watch out for the Ambitious Mum; husband long-since died of exhaustion providing all the glamorous trappings and status symbols she craves. Her daughter-in-law must be a status symbol also, and RICH - so *NEVER* be seduced into opening a joint bank account. Start wearing Gucci shoes and talk with a plum in your mouth to practise the Correct Accent. Or give up.

Mum's of the Prudish and Pernickety type? Home kept like a hospital? Tidies your drawers *after* you've tided them? Explains carefully how to hang up the bath-towel? Your man probably washes behind his ears at least twice a day, and likes the crease in his trousers to go right up to his waist. May even expect to have his underpants ironed. Watch it! Mum is probably highly sexually frustrated herself, and doesn't see why anyone else should enjoy themselves. You may even have to teach your man How To Do It.

Mums come in all shapes and sizes and all temperaments. They can be workers, intellectuals, matriarchs, political activists, dappy, promiscuous, do-gooders, man-substitutes, ambitious status-seekers, traditional cuddlies, recluses, flappers, boozers, sluts, socialites, business executives, organisers, jolly, prudish and pernickety, or just Everybody's Mum. Most are quite safe, some are thoroughly enjoyable - but some can be downright dangerous.

MOTHERS

If your man has a geriatric mum, pack your bags and get ready to move - and establish contact immediately with an amenable doctor, unless you want to take a crash course in nursing. The move-in-mum can be fine, especially if well-trained and loves Doing Chores - but take care of territorial encroachment and the second-time-around mother/grandmother syndrome. For the intellectual mum, study your man's newspapers rapaciously and swat up on your Balzac. Prepare yourself for long sessions of brain stretching, when you will never be in the right.

Even the seemingly safe-as-houses traditional mums need a bit of care. Make sure you *wear* those dreadful hand-knitted woollies on every possible occasion, and steel yourself for a huge weepy white wedding with armies of aunts.

All Things Can Be Handled. Just approach with much care, and observe closely for any tell-tale signs. But if you're genuinely keen on your man and want to hang on-to him, Mum must think you're *marvellous* (or as marvellous as can be expected) - so act accordingly.

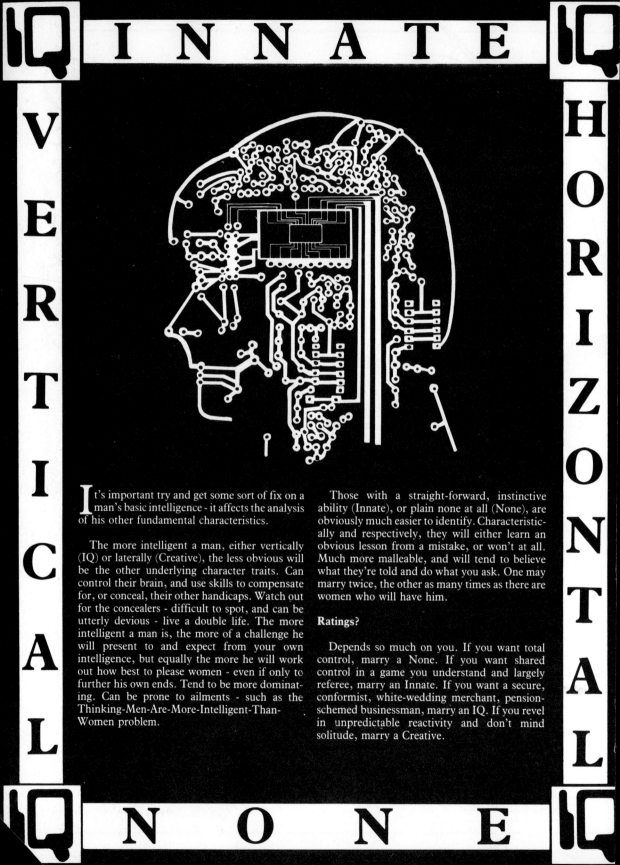

It's important try and get some sort of fix on a man's basic intelligence - it affects the analysis of his other fundamental characteristics.

The more intelligent a man, either vertically (IQ) or laterally (Creative), the less obvious will be the other underlying character traits. Can control their brain, and use skills to compensate for, or conceal, their other handicaps. Watch out for the concealers - difficult to spot, and can be utterly devious - live a double life. The more intelligent a man is, the more of a challenge he will present to and expect from your own intelligence, but equally the more he will work out how best to please women - even if only to further his own ends. Tend to be more dominating. Can be prone to ailments - such as the Thinking-Men-Are-More-Intelligent-Than-Women problem.

Those with a straight-forward, instinctive ability (Innate), or plain none at all (None), are obviously much easier to identify. Characteristically and respectively, they will either learn an obvious lesson from a mistake, or won't at all. Much more malleable, and will tend to believe what they're told and do what you ask. One may marry twice, the other as many times as there are women who will have him.

Ratings?

Depends so much on you. If you want total control, marry a None. If you want shared control in a game you understand and largely referee, marry an Innate. If you want a secure, conformist, white-wedding merchant, pension-schemed businessman, marry an IQ. If you revel in unpredictable reactivity and don't mind solitude, marry a Creative.

THIS IS
GREY MATTER

TRY THIS ON HIM:

If making love for thirty minutes consumes the same amount of energy as running 4 miles, and playing with himself is the equivalent of running 2 miles, and a mile is the equivalent of £1.00 value of food/weight loss, and he earns £10,000 per annum before tax at 32½%, owns a car, has a wife and two children at private school, a mortgage of £25,000 at 12% interest and wants to install a swimming pool and breed cockatoos . . .

. . . How many times a year can he afford to make love before everyone starves to death?

A: 1½ times!

VIRILITY

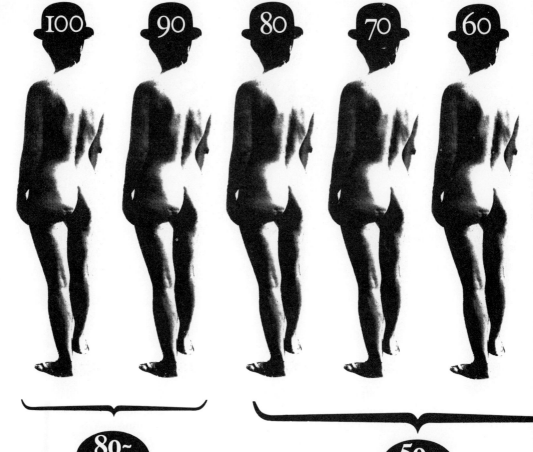

81-100% Male hormones

Very bullish and aggressive. Want to lead. Pushers and shovers. Spend much time in clubs and on golf-courses yahooing. Boring. Insensitive. Treat women like chattels and send kids to military camps. Extremely full of their own importance, which they vest in themselves. Laugh loud and long at their own jokes; rugger-buggers.

Rating: **AVOID**   0

51-80% Male hormones

Definitely men, but on the aggressive side. Pushy and rather demanding; tend to prefer male groupings. Slightly inconsiderate at times; sporty; extrovert and enjoy a good laugh. Not particularly creative; able and persistent; conformist.

Rating: **FINE**   8

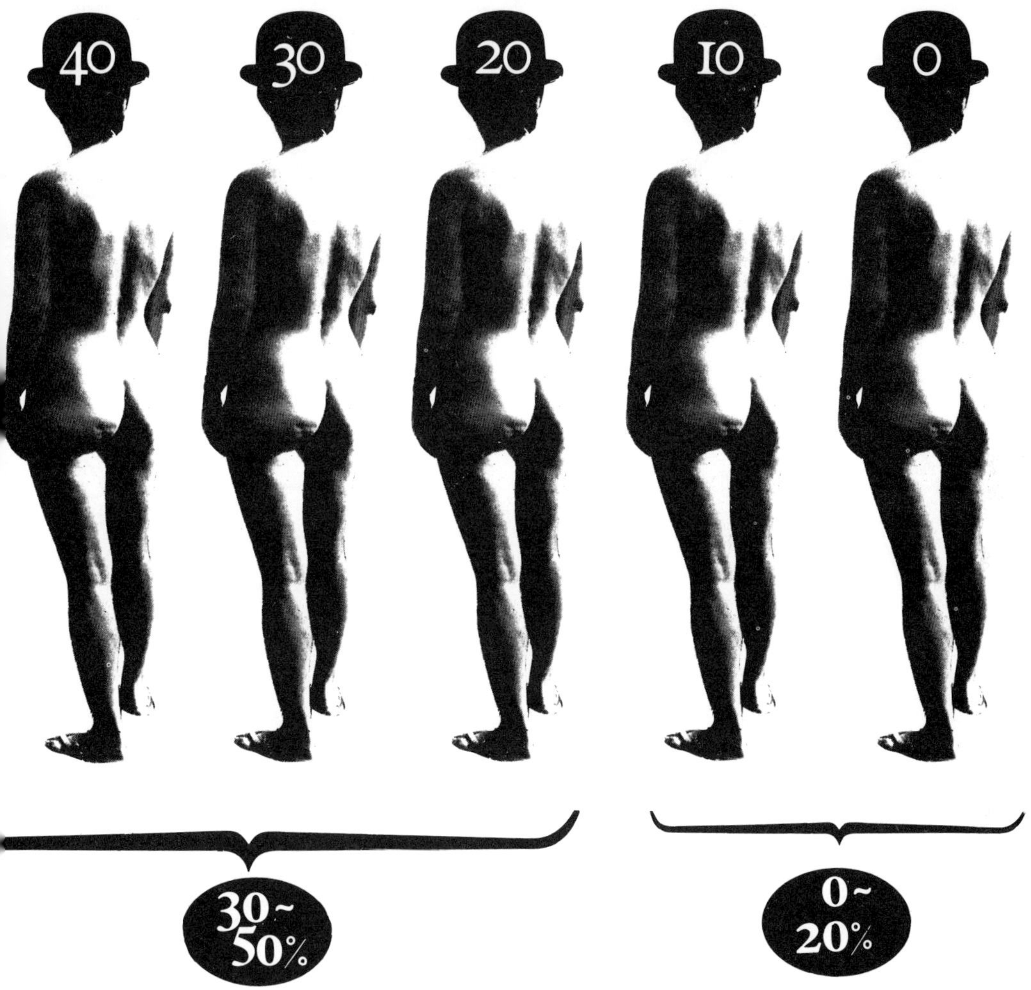

21-50% Male hormones

Definitely men, but on the gentle side; slightly fussy. Sensitive, intellectual; often creative; understanding and thoughtful towards women. Take a while to get to know; romantic; caring - sometimes loners. Not keen on male groups. Tend to feel slightly inferior at times.

Rating: SPLENDID 10

1-20% Male hormones

Effeminate to very effeminate. Nearly women - almost hermaphrodite. Could be transvestite or transexual. Often Gay. If go for women at all, go for the boy-girls, the straight-up-and-downers. Delicate, sensitive, cultured and often creative. Get on well with women - like them without necessarily wanting them. Often intelligent and moody.

Rating: RISKY 2

VIRILITY

A subject of all-consuming concern and interest to men . . .

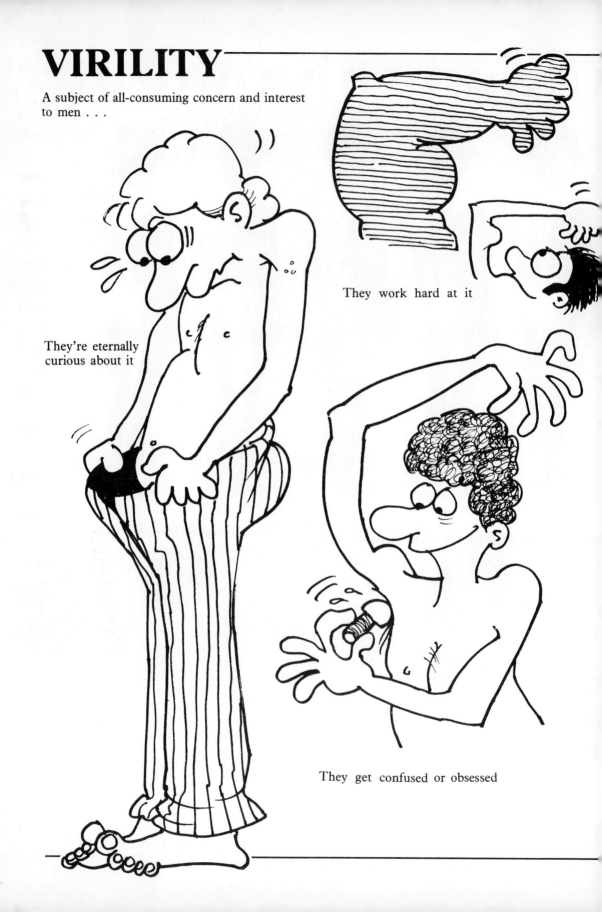

They work hard at it

They're eternally curious about it

They get confused or obsessed

Or panicky

Or pernickety

Or dire

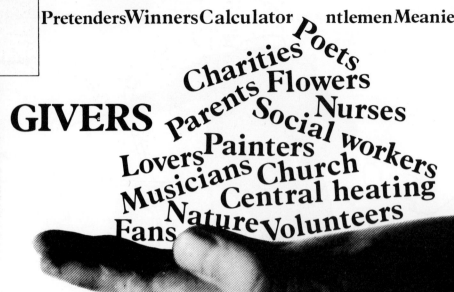

GIVERS

Charities Poets
Parents Flowers
Lovers Painters Nurses
Musicians Church Social workers
Fans Nature Volunteers Central heating

Givers

Usually warm and secure people at ease with themselves and the world. Careful, hard-working, rather incautious. Bad at assessing other personalities. Tend to be sitting ducks for con-men. Good listeners, thoughtful and tender. These are the natural instinctive givers. Beware the contrived givers, who give to create an impression and further their aims. Usually a sinister Taker in camouflage. Caution also with the compulsive givers - prone to suffocate you under mountains of chocolates and red roses, regardless of what *you* actually like. Rather brash and insensitive, but essentially mean well, and harmless. The genuine, gentle givers make smashing lovers, fathers and friends, but be prepared for a life full of Waifs and Strays.

Rating: **If you're a taker**   **10**
Rating: **If you're a giver**   **8**

TAKERS

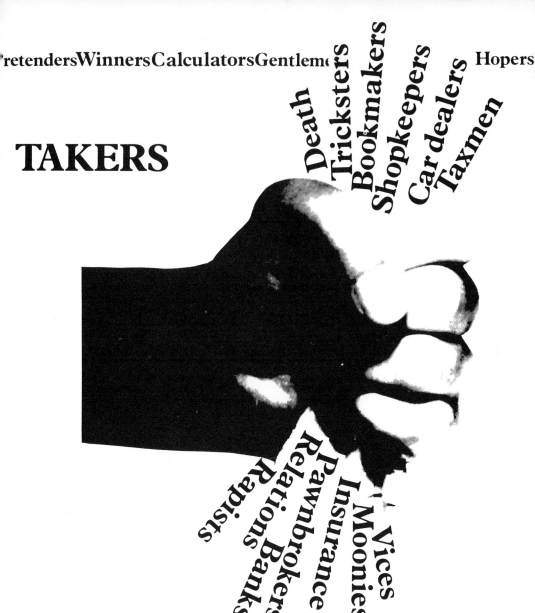

Death Tricksters Bookmakers Shopkeepers Car dealers Taxmen

Rapists Banks Relations Pawnbrokers Insurance Pararce Moonies Vices

Takers

Usually wind up in such professions as commerce, banking, law, insurance, charitable institutions, Inland Revenue, pension funds and the Church. People who are geared to receive, or take or, at the worst extremes, grab and steal. Well-balanced takers will need overt expressions of love and security of possessions. Natural manipulators; methodical and well-organised. Predictable. Slightly naive and insecure. To further extremes, they are highly demanding of time, attention and all material things, especially money. Greed born of insecurity often drives them to great prosperity and well-publicised charitable acts. Will tend to make rather callous lovers - if *they're* in The Mood, that's fine by them. Equally, won't necessarily notice if you have a fling on the side to compensate.

Rating:	If you're a giver	8
Rating:	If you're a taker	2

GIVERS&TAKERS

"Take this! Have that!
Please . . . Just a little
something . . .
Oh, do say you'll accept!
I'll pay!
Take me!"

"Listen! I've taken just about as much as I can have!"

PRESENTATION

PEACOCK

CHAMELEO

Peacocks

Instantly spottable. Wear jewellery and grow beards. Desperately insecure and fundamentally weak. Know that by decorating themselves with flamboyant clothes and flowery gestures they are instantly non-threatening to groupies and won't be expected to compete. Love flattery. Often very sad, nervy people. Can tend to attract other men by mistake, and slide into unintentional homosexuality. Depressive, hypochondriac, twitchy, inconsistent and selfish. Brashness conceals deep sadness. The court-jesters of Life.

Tend to marry ugly women who pose no threat to them as the main ornaments in life.

Rating: DIRE   **0**

Chameleons

The role players - another small and difficult group to spot. Appearance carefully devised to blend into any background, and will be conscious-groupies on occasions, pretending to be a real groupie so as not to threaten the group

CIVIL SERVANTS · LAWYERS · STOCKBROKERS · RELIGIOUS · INSURANCE · COWBOYS · ART DIRECTORS · PUNKS · COUNTY · POLICE · MILITARY · HOMO SEX

GROUPY

who find true individuals unsettling. Never advertise their presence - are the true loners in life. Often shy, creative, deep-thinking, clever to the point of being cunning. Can even find a family environment restrictive, frustrating and claustrophobic. Build fences at the bottom of the garden and go for long walks with the dog. Find it hard to relax - restless. Dislike formality. Responsible and probably instinctively faithful, but can be lured away by other women who find them too fascinating to resist. Have you got the degree of understanding he requires - if you can spot him in the first place?

Rating: HIGHLY DESIRABLE   10

Groupies

By far the largest section. Most men will fall into affinity groups of like-minded and like-dressed men. Derive much of their strength, security and personality make-up from the group. All groupies in isolation are more

PRESENTATION

susceptible to domination by women. Society encourages the formation of groups, and most groupies are traditionalists. A groupie in his group is safe, smug, and feels more powerful.

The addict-groupie

Most groupies are of the addict variety; those who are genuinely weak outside the group environment. Predictable and consistent - because they can't help it. Prepare for plenty of reunions, club outings, evenings in the pub, old-boy ties, parties and predictable package holidays. Solid and unembarrassing. Exclusive and rather selfish. Tend to wear instantly-recognisable uniforms - pin-stripes, punk gear, police uniform etc. Run all the secret societies. Find true individuals a threat to their secure conformity.

Rating: SAFE ENOUGH   7

The conscious-groupie

Those who choose to join a group only when and where it suits them are genuinely strong and together men, who will be very successful. Join groups not because they like them, but as a means to promote their own success. Shrewd and suprising. There aren't very many about, and make sure they're difficult to recognise. If you spot him - congratulations! You've a highly individual man.

Rating: A WINNER   10

PRESENTATION (beards)

FATHER CHRISTMAS OR KARL MARX

The majority of men who sport beards fall into the Peacock group - ornamenting themselves helps them to establish their identity and assists their careers, especially those who trim them very neatly and artistically. Some men grow beards through sheer laziness - beware the slob. Some in an attempt to look older - they may grow out of it. Some to hide weak chins - the insecure. Some to state their identity - a kind of uniform - such as anarchists and revolutionaries. And some - a minority - just allow all that hair to sprout and run riot simply because they feel thoroughly comfortable and at ease that way. But as a general rule, the sight of a beard should arouse your suspicions - investigate further.

BUILD

Middling Men

Neither one thing nor the other. Handicapped by lack of motivation - just plain Normal. Not particularly liked by other men. Will succeed moderatcly, as tend to be conscious grafters, so not so much time to go out and play the field.

Short men

Underlying all character traits of short men rests their fundamental hatred of Being Short. Often try to disguise lack of height with platform soles, a springy stride, and as bouffant hair-styles as they can manage. This, plus the fact that they tend to wear loud clothes and talk fast and flamboyantly can lead one to suppose they are slightly effeminate. They usually aren't - quite the opposite. Sexually aggressive to compensate for seeming shortage of manhood. Rather pushy or extrovert. Used to fending for themselves;

slightly defensive - anything to overcome innate feeling of inferiority. Often become actors or salesmen; can be extremely successful in business. If you're very short or extremely tall, you'll be a bee-line target for short men.

Rating: TO BE WATCHED   **2**

Make sound, dependable husbands, if rather unimaginative lovers. Won't get to the top in business, but chances are won't be unfaithful either. Good, solid family men. Plodders. Grow vegetables.

Rating: SOUNDLY DULL   **5**

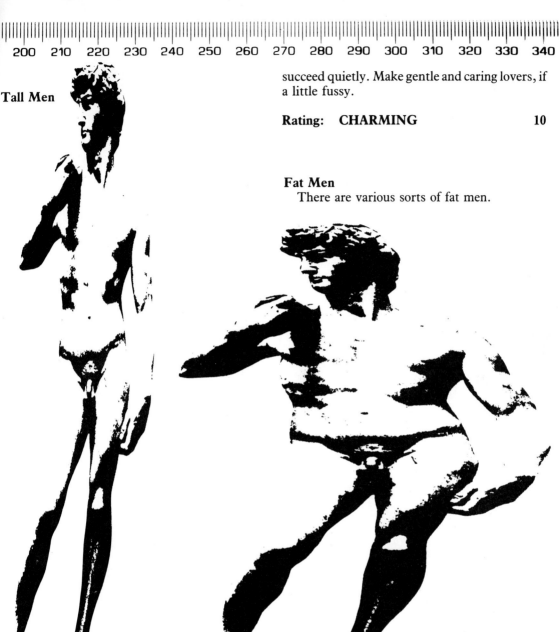

Tall Men

succeed quietly. Make gentle and caring lovers, if a little fussy.

Rating: **CHARMING** **10**

Fat Men

There are various sorts of fat men.

Generally embarrassed by etiolated, beanpole growth as youths - leads to tendency to be slightly hunched. Quietly spoken, shy and deferential. Cautious - ever-mindful of low doorways. Can be rather particular, especially in selection of seats in cinemas, etc. Often do well in the entrenched world of business; cannot fail to be noticed and

The Fatty-fatty

Historically, fatness represented success and opulence. Other men instinctively respect them. Often very mother-dominated - always being fed up to grow into a Big Strong Boy. Food more exciting than women, so eat rather than make love. Very career-orientated, and often rather

BUILD

sad, though superficially jolly. Great if you want everything on a grand scale and a sex-free life.

Rating: DEBATABLE   2

The Middle-fatty

Comfortably podgy. Get on well in business versus thin men, as pose less of a threat to upper management. Very bright, often highly devious. Use physical form to give impression of safe affability, but really manipulating their size to further their business or sexual career. Tend to be rather selfish. Very successful in bed - when

you're least expecting to have arrived there. Number One man in the world to Watch Out For. As a husband - great, if you want lots of money, power and status symbols, but the price can be turning a blind eye to infidelity.

Rating: CAUTIOUSLY OPTIMISTIC 8

COLLECTOR

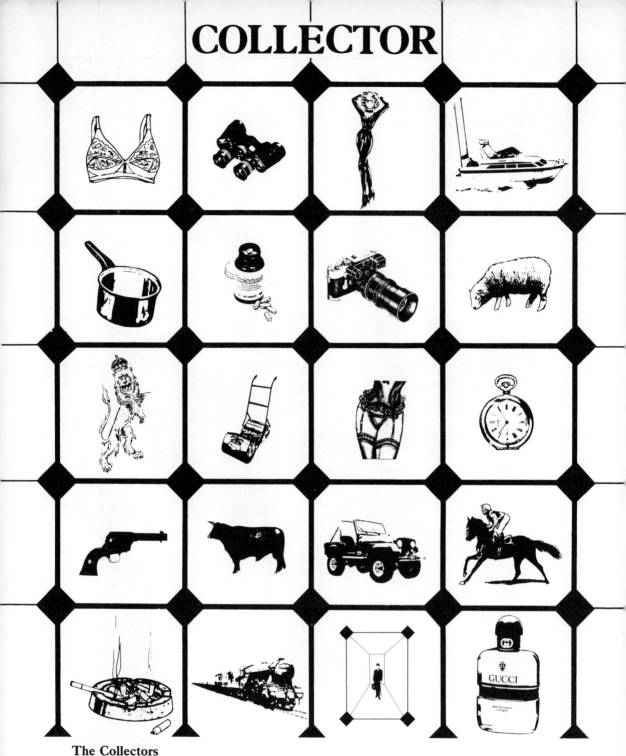

The Collectors

Will always be adding to their collection, be it money, possessions or women. Tend to view women as another sort of possession. Will dominate the home environment. Unless women are the objects of their collecting mania, tend to be very faithful, even predictable. Remember birthdays and anniversaries. To excess, can become bores, with endless home movies and family snap-shots. Carry pictures of the family and umpteen visiting cards in their wallets. Collect friends and like entertaining at home. Extrovert. Tend to untidiness - not too bothered about appearance. Lose socks. Irreligious. Variable. Very British. Hate change - especially moving house - too much hassle moving all those collections. Need a very tolerant and ordered woman.

Rating: **If you're a non-collector** 10
Rating: **If you're a collector** 2

NON~COLLECTOR

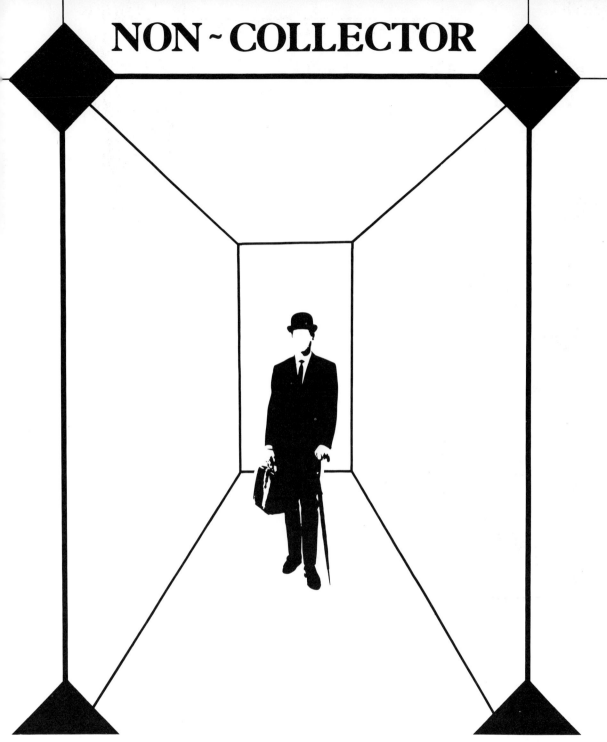

The Non-Collectors

The aesthetes. Any collection you may have, forget it. Jealous, particular, loners. Like living simply, even spartanly. Enjoy travelling and taking ladies to the opera. Tend to be shy, selfish, slightly narcissistic and introspective, but single-minded, clear-thinking and analytical. Would never make Mastermind. Don't want to assume any fixed sort of identity, and build protective walls around themselves to stave off deep human contact. Threatened by large groups of men. Incapable of public speaking, acting or singing. Can tend to neurosis and breakdowns and hypochondria. Likely to meditate, do yoga and jog. Generally less happy and fulfilled than the collectors. Need a very understanding and homely woman.

| Rating: | If you're a collector | 8 |
| Rating: | If you're a non-collector | 0 |

COLLECTORS &
NON~COLLECTORS

Both collectors and non-collectors consume space: one to store all his junk in – the other to sit and contemplate in.

TRAIN SETS

STAMPS

BOOKS

BUTTERF

MATCHSTICK BUILDERS

TOY SOLDIERS

FOREIGN COINS

BOTTLES

LOVE LETTERS

KNICKER COLLECTORS

How to score

It's only by learning how to score accurately that you will progress in the art of Man-Spotting.

The first section of the book dealt with the fundamental characteristics and scored each notable section as a 'classic case' with ratings from 0 to 10.

The following pages contain carefully selected examples of some standard and not-so-standard species that have been spotted and which are felt to be varied and representative enough to provide a sound grounding for the spotter's analysis. Interspersed among the basic characters are various comments and observations about habits, habitat, behavioural idiosyncrasies, etc.

Aligned with each Character is a score chart. He is open to your own analysis of how he might be rated in relation to the fundamental scores originally supplied, and you can score him accordingly as you think appropriate. At the back of the book (p.156-7) are the Experts' scores for you to check against.

The tenth rating feature - Odds & Ends - is left open to your own interpretation. There are so many, many variations, and the scope from the highly offensive to the vastly entertaining is so broad - and so subjective - that only your own experience and tolerance levels can decide.

Opposite is an example of how one of the characters might be scored, and what the final outcome implies. You are encouraged to approach the other characters in the book in the same way and keep checking your results with the ones ultimately provided. Whilst it is possible to attempt the scoring from the clues surrounding each character, to perfect your scoring ability you are best advised to go out into the field, hunt them down, get to know them, and *then* see how your scoring fares. If nothing else, it'll certainly widen your circle of male acquaintances.

STANDARD WARNING
No man is actually perfect, but there are levels of acceptability and non-acceptability. If a man scores below 50 in your reckoning, think twice. Anyone who scores below 35 - RUN - fast - now.

He's done alright for
himself . . .
(State Co-Ed.)

Education

What a cheerful Charlie . . .
(largely Sanguine)

Character

Here's a Nice Clean
Boy . . .
(Matriarchal Mum)

Mother

Obviously has street sense –
knows his onions . . .
(Innate – should complement
my IQ)

Intellect

Nice hair cut . . .
(Sensitive)

Virility

Something of an honest
thief, I'd say . . .
(Taker – Okay, I'm a giver)

Giver/Taker

Jolly dapper – like
the bow tie. Acceptable,
though . . .
(Peacock)

Presentation

Hmm. A little on the
short side . . .
(Natural salesman)

Build

Just look at all those
cars . . .
(Collector – Whoops, so am I)

**Collector/
Non Collector**

Twitchy and show-offy.
Undoubtedly habit-ridden . . .

Odds n'Ends

Urgers
Hopers
Gentlemen
Soapers
Hummers
Og
Scruffs
Dunces
Loners
Dancers
ers
Nudgers
Sweeties

You could
marry one of these...

Kinkies
Yel
wers
Flashers
Animals
Eaters
Feelies
Zom
Joggers
Voters
Chasers
Junkies
Ramblers
Failures
Singers
Neckers
Intend
ctuals
Sweeties
Approachers
Calculators
Fakers
Commies
Uglies
Elbowers
Booz
Jerks
Lovers
Belchers
Queens
Artists
Gamblers
Doers
Winners
Nudists
Mix
Meanies
Bastards
Tweekies
Pretenders
Hicks
Pu
Yes-men
Losers
Rowdies
Moodies
sers

The characters

In later life . . .

Still lying about his age – and everything else, for that matter.

Could be . . .

IZZY, OZZI, JACOB, ALF, DES, KEN, MATT

Education 10

Character 10

Mother 10

Intellect 10

Virility 10

Giver/Taker 10

Presentation 10

Build 10

Collector/ Non Collector 10

Odds n'Ends 10

 100

In later life ...

Still ranting and raving and promoting The Revolution, but still refuses to emigrate and leave the rest of us in peace. Leading from the rear – knows how to play safe.

Could be ...

GASTON, AUBREY, CLIVE, SINBAD, ALEX, LENNY, IVAN

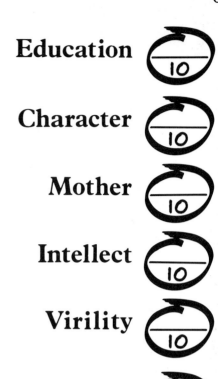

Education 10

Character 10

Mother 10

Intellect 10

Virility 10

Giver/Taker 10

Presentation 10

Build 10

Collector/ Non Collector 10

Odds and Ends 10

100

In later life . . .

Totally rutted. Dreaming of the Empire. Talks about colonialism and exporting convicts.

Could be . . .

EDWARD, CHARLES, ANDREW, PHILIP, WILLIAM, HENRY

Education 10

Character 10

Mother 10

Intellect 10

Virility 10

Giver/Taker 10

Presentation 10

Build 10

Collector/ Non Collector 10

Odds n'Ends 10

 100

SLEEPING HABITS

This section obviously presupposes that your relationship has progressed to a certain level of intimacy and familiarity, but it has to be considered seriously if you are intending to formalise your partnership For Better or For Worse.

Whilst sleeping habits may not necessarily reveal astounding and profound insights into your man's character, they will affect you - so forewarned to be single-bedded. Some sleeping habits are downright offensive - such as bedwetting, or sleeping with the family pets. Some just may not suit you - and really this depends on you. You'll find the fresh-air fiends, and the fug-lovers; the naked apes, and those who need masses of clothes and bedclothes; those who have to have the light on and the door open and MUST sleep on their side of the bed; more entertainingly (perhaps) - the sleepwalkers. If you're determined he's your man, you'll doubtless find ways of contriving how best to sleep together, but here are a few Standards:

The Starfish

The attitude of a man at ease, spreadeagled all over the bed - and all over you. Usually a placid enough sleeper, not easily woken. You can probably wrap one limp arm around *you* for a cuddle without disturbing his slumbers, or the intermittent gurgly snores. A generous partner.

The Log

Dead to the world. Usually passes out the instant he's finished making love, flat on his back, with reverberating snores to follow soon after. Feel if you Like It in the middle of the night. Extreme cases may lead you to consider separate bedrooms and soundproofing. Usually not the most considerate of men - or lovers. If you're desperate, try sewing a tennis ball into the back of his pyjamas.

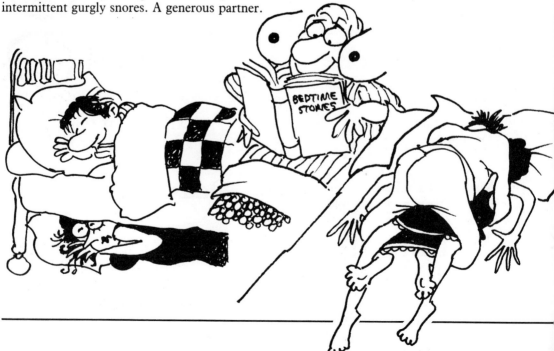

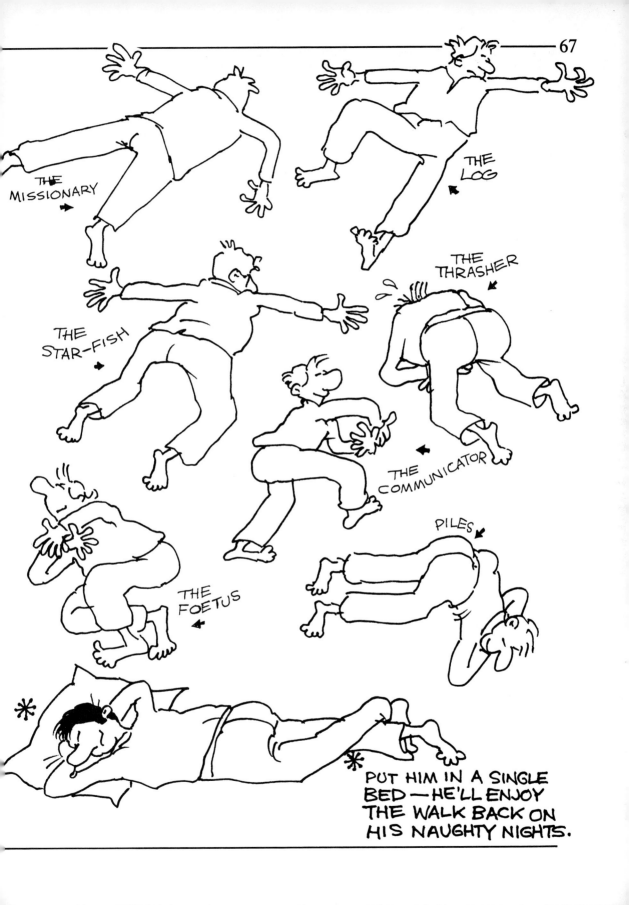

SLEEPING HABITS

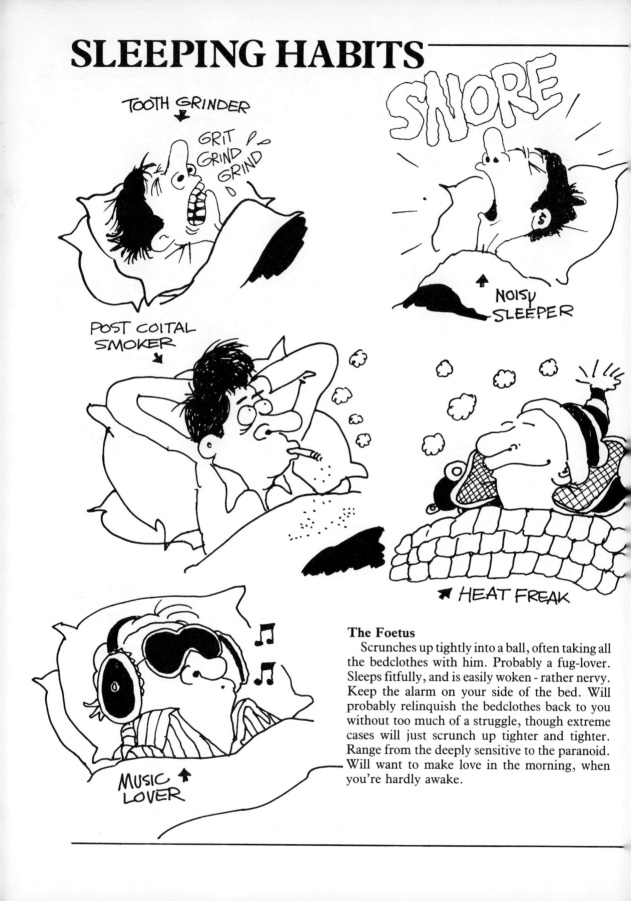

TOOTH GRINDER

GRIT GRIND GRIND

SNORE

NOISY SLEEPER

POST COITAL SMOKER

HEAT FREAK

MUSIC LOVER

The Foetus
    Scrunches up tightly into a ball, often taking all the bedclothes with him. Probably a fug-lover. Sleeps fitfully, and is easily woken - rather nervy. Keep the alarm on your side of the bed. Will probably relinquish the bedclothes back to you without too much of a struggle, though extreme cases will just scrunch up tighter and tighter. Range from the deeply sensitive to the paranoid. Will want to make love in the morning, when you're hardly awake.

PET LOVER

SLEEP WALKER

FOOT FIDGET

The Thrasher

Oh boy. Demolishes the bed every night - and never offers to help make it. Much grinding of teeth and flailing arms and legs. Dreams volubly, if unintelligibly, and tends to throw bedclothes off the bed completely rather than grab them. If you don't need much sleep and don't mind a few bruises, fine. Could be the devious sort - conscience troubling him?

The Communicator

Needs human contact and falls asleep all wrapped around you. Deeply affectionate, and possibly slightly insecure. Extreme cases will fall into the sleeping with the light on and surrounded by pets category. Basically, though, if you're a fairly quiet sleeper and can cope with occasional suffocation, a lovely, cosy partner.

In later life . . .

Merciless in business. Married rich – has done anything and everything to accumulate and hang on to MONEY. Goes to hairdresser and body masseur once a week. A voyeur. Takes vitamin pills.

Could be . . .

GEOFF, PATRICK, IVAN, OSCAR, CRISPIN, RODNEY, PIERS

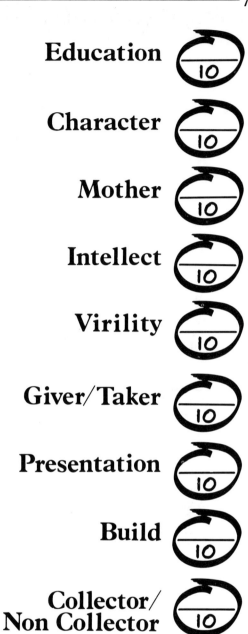

Education — 10

Character — 10

Mother — 10

Intellect — 10

Virility — 10

Giver/Taker — 10

Presentation — 10

Build — 10

Collector/Non Collector — 10

Odds n'Ends — 10

100

In later life . . .

Knocked down and run over leaving the pub late one night. The newspaper he worked on never reported it – probably don't even realise he's dead.

Could be . . .

SANDY, VIVIEN, CARROL, LESLIE, FRANCIS, AUBREY, ADRIAN

Education

Character

Mother

Intellect

Virility

Giver/Taker

Presentation

Build

Collector/ Non Collector

Odds n'Ends

In later life . . .

Badly crippled – has been knee-capped, knuckled and knackered. Still well-connected in certain circles. Keeper of his Manor – lives in a very high-rise east-end flat – free of charge.

Could be . . .

CRAIG, RONNIE, CLIFF, BUSTER, BUTCH, DANNY, DEAN, CY

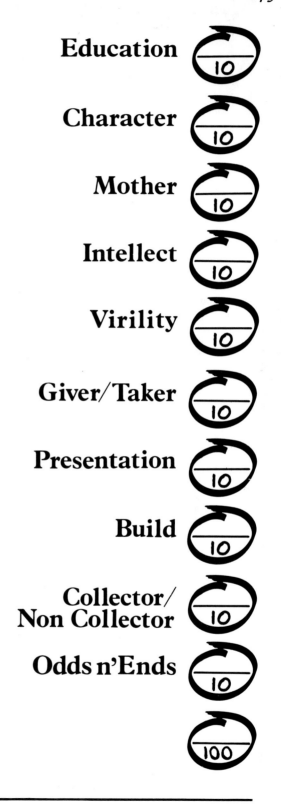

Education — 10

Character — 10

Mother — 10

Intellect — 10

Virility — 10

Giver/Taker — 10

Presentation — 10

Build — 10

Collector/Non Collector — 10

Odds n'Ends — 10

— 100

NASTY HABITS

All men are habit-ridden. Some are tolerable, some less so, and you can usually do something about the more irritable or offensive ones - once you know the cause.

Most habits are born of either Natural Filth, or Natural Insecurity, the former obviously being easier both to spot and to deal with. These include the scratch-scratch and pick-pick variety, and we would suggest a programme of bathing together to be beneficial. Carefully selected un-birthday presents can also make constructive inroads.

The fiddle-fiddle variety indicate a tense nervousness and basic insecurity - especially with other objects. Fiddling with parts of the anatomy can also reflect a need in him to reassure himself that he is Still All There and intact. He may well be a married man, especially if his fiddling tends to become more frenzied at particular times of the evening. He may simply be in need of emotional comfort and security.

Scruffy, unparticular and even down-right dirty men will tend to perform their habits quite happily and openly in public, so they are easy to spot. The superficially immaculate man can be dangerous, and requires more intimate scrutiny in the privacy of a domestic environment. The secretive fiddler may be more comfortable to go out and about with in public, but he's usually more complex, and could even be more sinister, than the overtly habit-ridden man.

In later life . . .

VISITORS ONLY

Made a profession of escaping – and being caught again, giggling. Basically means no harm. A nuisance.

Could be . . .

ALGERNON, SIGMUND, CONRAD, QUENTIN, MYCROFT, PATERSHALL, WILBERFORCE

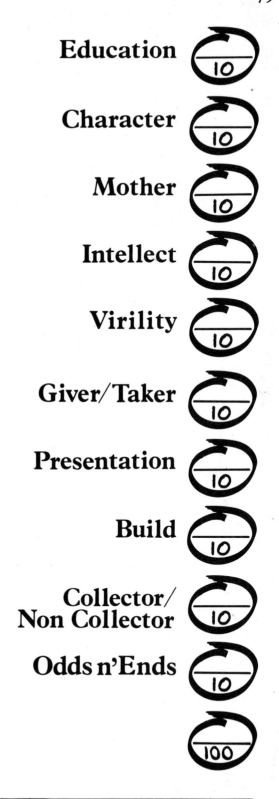

Education — 10

Character — 10

Mother — 10

Intellect — 10

Virility — 10

Giver/Taker — 10

Presentation — 10

Build — 10

Collector/Non Collector — 10

Odds n' Ends — 10

— 100

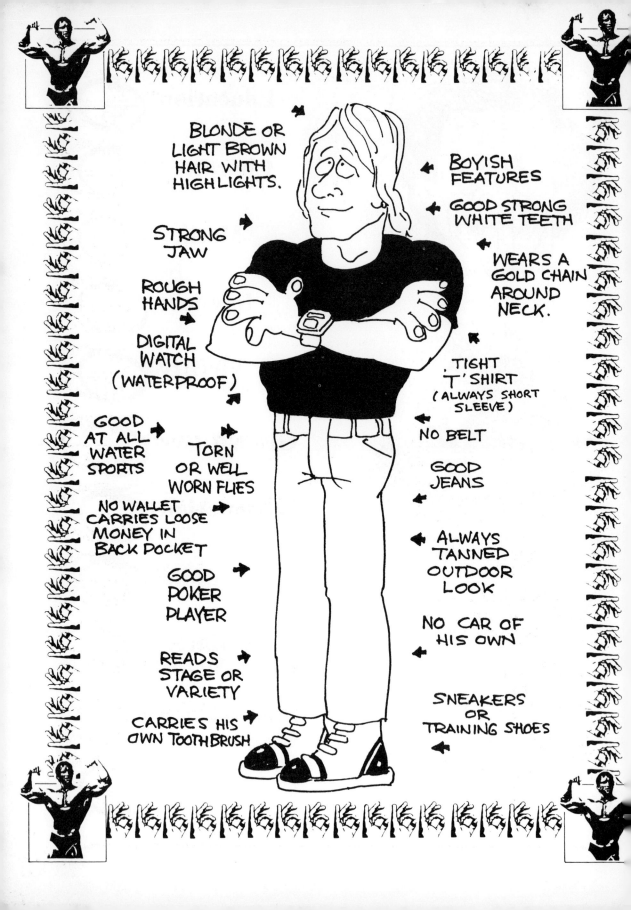

In later life . . .

Has married money, if he's lucky. Spends much time puffing pipes, putting on golfing greens and sailing. Surprisingly obedient.

Could be . . .

GARY, KEVIN, STEVE, HANK, BRUCE, BARRY, CHUCK

Education 10

Character 10

Mother 10

Intellect 10

Virility 10

Giver/Taker 10

Presentation 10

Build 10

Collector/ Non Collector 10

Odds n'Ends 10

 100

DRIVES
VINTAGE
MOTORCYCLE

FOOTBALL
SUPPORTER

DRINKS
ONLY REAL
ALE

HI-FI
FREAK

HAS
CB IN
CAR

TELEVISION
OR VIDEO
MECHANIC

INTO
COUNTRY
&
WESTERN
MUSIC

READS
SCIENCE
FICTION

HAS
PEN
PAL

SHOPS
AT C&A

STILL
LIVES WITH
PARENTS

ALWAYS
SEEN IN A
GROUP OF
MALE FRIENDS

VERY GENEROUS

In later life . . .

Started pub business with brother – doing alternate nights. Very jolly and bluff. Still plays Acker Bilk and Rosemary Clooney records.

Could be . . .

GUS, DANNY, GERALD, PAT, DONOVAN, SEAN, GRAHAM

Education 10

Character 10

Mother 10

Intellect 10

Virility 10

Giver/Taker 10

Presentation 10

Build 10

Collector/ Non Collector 10

Odds n'Ends 10

 100

DISGUSTING HABITS

Y ou only have to overhear schoolboys giggling behind the sheds to know what all this is about. A large number of men really do have quite alarmingly disgusting habits. Many of them you may never know about, since they're rather shameful things and tend therefore to be carried out ceremoniously behind locked doors. You may not want to know about them - in which case turn the page immediately. Generally speaking, all disgusting habits are quite unnecessary. You may introduce a negative system of rating here.

Peeing in basins:
Denotes a weak bladder, or someone who's too bone idle to walk down the hotel corridor to the lavatory. Also goes for peeing out of windows. Nasty.

SCRATCH
SCRATCH

Extended sit-ins:
Could be constipated - shovel roughage down him, and hope. Or total selfishness; or revels in lavatorial odours. Move out.

The big thrust:
Pathetic display of grossly assumed genitalia - hang-back to the days of penis-gourds and cod pieces. Probably conceals a serious deficiency in this area. Italians most notable exponents of the art-form - haunt swimming pools. Homosexuals often eschew underpants to allow maximum expression of their genitalia through artfully faded jeans. Don't laugh - it's rather sad.

Peeing in the bath:
   Could be a repeat of the weak bladder/no lavatory *or* sink syndrome. Or could denote an amniotic fluid adoration - likes feeling of being warmly and wetly surrounded. Bath separately.

Bed-farting:
   May be the result of too may beers, beans and curries; hideous if a combination of all three - watch his diet - controllable. Or a sign of increasing age. Move to a separate bedroom.

There are many, many more too numerous - or too downright disgusting - to mention, some of which are shown here. For further information, see also 'Bathroom Habits'.

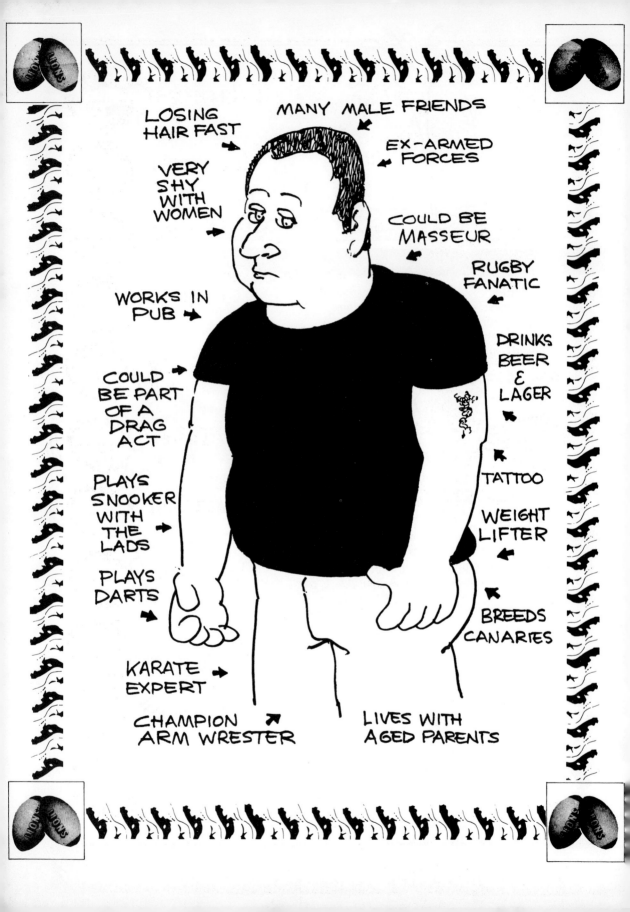

In later life . . .

Ever since he did GBH for throwing a bag of cement at someone, has been the most peaceable soul you could ever meet.

Could be . . .

SID, BERT, RON, ALF, PETE, LENNY, DES

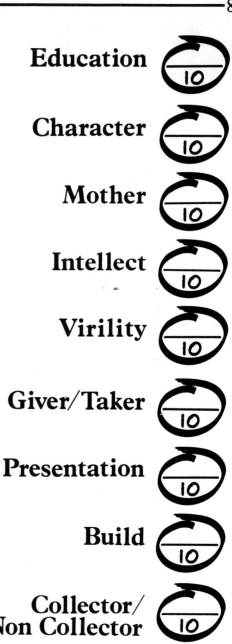

Education ⟨10⟩

Character ⟨10⟩

Mother ⟨10⟩

Intellect ⟨10⟩

Virility ⟨10⟩

Giver/Taker ⟨10⟩

Presentation ⟨10⟩

Build ⟨10⟩

Collector/ Non Collector ⟨10⟩

Odds n'Ends ⟨10⟩

⟨100⟩

In later life . . .

Now a night-club owner. Dodgy – well into the black economy. Has 5 overseas bank accounts. Manages to stay legal – just.

Could be . . .

KEVIN, MARVIN, IRVINE, MAURICE, VICTOR, GERRY

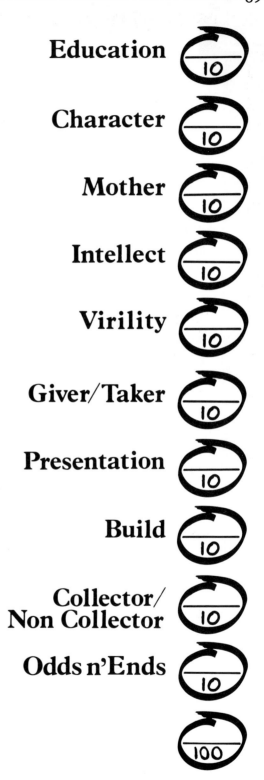

Education 10

Character 10

Mother 10

Intellect 10

Virility 10

Giver/Taker 10

Presentation 10

Build 10

Collector/ Non Collector 10

Odds n'Ends 10

100

In later life . . .

Increasingly crotchety. Still toting the same old folio around. Has corns on backs of heels from putting feet on stereo equipment and desks. Idle. A poseur. Thinks every idea is his.

Could be . . .

MARTIN, CHRISTOPHER, COLIN, ANDREW, MICHAEL, ADRIAN, CARL

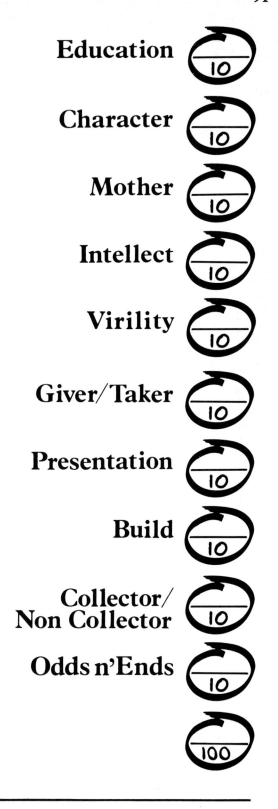

Education 10

Character 10

Mother 10

Intellect 10

Virility 10

Giver/Taker 10

Presentation 10

Build 10

Collector/ Non Collector 10

Odds n'Ends 10

100

BATHROOM HABITS

Bathrooms. Those traditional havens of privacy where All Sorts of Things go on. Probably best to leave him to it. If you *have* to go in there, take the radio with you, and turn on the hot tap to generate lots of steam. Smoking cigars can also help.

What will you find your man doing in there? Well . . .

Fiddling with himself in front of the mirror - totally absorbed; preening, posing, posturing, flexing his muscles, and looking at himself sideways out of the corners of his eyes; examining and picking his teeth; leaning out of the window, binoculars trained on the nude in the opposite bathroom; riddling dandruff out of his hair like a snow storm; secretly examining himself for any alarming nasties (sinister, that); screwing earwax out of his ears and gunge from between his toes; picking off dry skin from his heels & elbows; playing with and examining all parts of his anatomy; experimenting with your make-up and clothes (dangerous, that); plucking out hairs - sometimes eyebrows, sometimes pubic, usually white hairs from scalp; smelling his armpits; and more - ad nauseam.

Think of the letter P, and you've got bathrooms - the Place of Preening, Plucking, Posturing, Picking, Posing, Playing, Puking, Patting, Prancing, etc.. - Peculiar - it's the Pits.

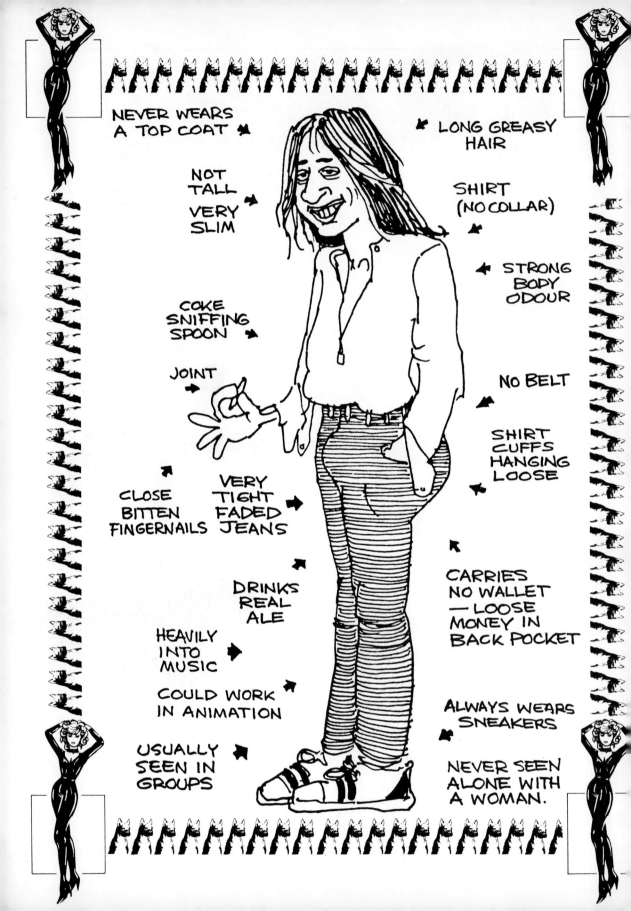

In later life . . .

Dead. Didn't mean to. Nobody cried.

Could be . . .

RICK, NEIL, BOBBY, HANK, KEITH, MARC, JIMI

Education 10

Character 10

Mother 10

Intellect 10

Virility 10

Giver/Taker 10

Presentation 10

Build 10

Collector/ Non Collector 10

Odds n'Ends 10

 100

DARK HAIR

SCHOOLBOY BASIN HAIRCUT

VERY SHORT SIGHTED

COLLECTS STAMPS

TAB OF SWEATER ALWAYS SHOWING

VERY MUCH INTO COMPUTERS

MARKS & SPARKS SWEATERS

READS A LOT (LIBRARY TICKET HOLDER)

GOOD CHURCH-GOER

MAKES MODEL CARS OR PLANES

HAS SECRET COLLECTION OF GIRLIE MAGAZINES

SCI-FI FILM BUFF

HAD HEALTH PROBLEMS AS A CHILD

WHEN MARRIED WILL SHARE HOME WITH MOTHER OR WIFE'S MOTHER.

RADIO HAM

EX-BOYS BRIGADE

In later life...

House bursting at the seams with gadgets and computers. Might still be a bachelor. Writes theses and lectures. Could live in Penge.

Could be...

CLIFFORD, SIMON, ANDREW, MARK, TIMOTHY, JOHNNIE, HUGH

Education

Character

Mother

Intellect

Virility

Giver/Taker

Presentation

Build

Collector/ Non Collector

Odds n'Ends

Education

Character

Mother

Intellect

Virility

Giver/Taker

Presentation

Build

Collector/
Non Collector

Odds and
Ends

In later life . . .

Already has a life peerage, and is Director of 5,000 Companies – all of which he's running into the ground through greed and incompetence. Plays golf most afternoons.

Could be . . .

JULIUS, GODFREY, CHRISTIAN, THOMAS, SAMUEL, PEREGRINE

RISK TAKERS & GAMBLERS

There are various sorts and degrees of risks, and various reasons behind them. Basically, some form of inadequacy, impotence, or sheer greed for money and power are behind all risks - and often, also, an aggressive and demanding woman. Equally, some degree of risk taking is necessary if a man is to succeed at all in life.

There is the schoolboy 'I dare you' risk - weak men trying to prove they're something they're not - be it brave, strong, sporty or rich. Insecure men; never really grew up or in an advanced stage of juvenile regression.

Naive risk-taking is acceptable in youth - they've got to learn somehow, and it shows they've got guts. When this continues into middle age - maybe too much successful risk-taking leading to addiction - you've got problems.

Unreasoned and compulsive risk-takers are dangerous and debilitating - he'll drag you down. You may need to get him to Gamblers Anonymous.

Intelligent and well-reasoned risk-taking in middle age is healthy and to be encouraged. But if an older man is still taking crazy risks - and more and more of them - then he's getting desperate. A classic case is the sixty-year-old who marries a twenty-year-old and thinks she's happy and faithful. We all know what usually happens.

And there are those who never take any risks. Terrifyingly boring and never really successful. Very dull lovers. Subside into early senility.

CITY STOCKBROKER

ALL BETS

MARATHON 1

AND THE BIGGEST GAMBLE OF ALL...

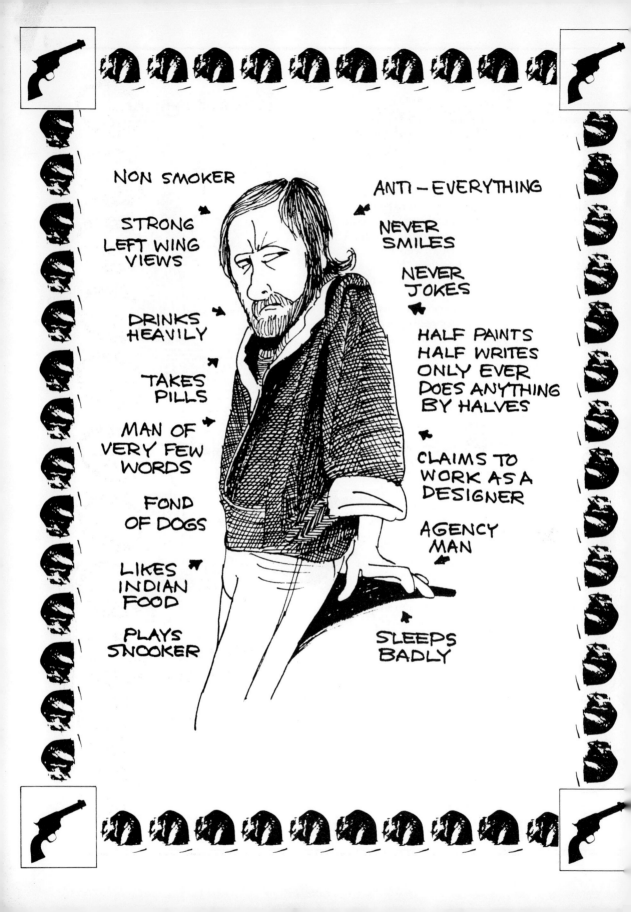

In later life . . .

Writes Trotskiist tracts. Not averse to bribery. Holidays in Cuba with well-known Miner's leader. Phones radio talk shows and won't shut up. Sells revolutionary newspapers outside stations and looks angry. Always has plenty of money.

Could be . . .

ART, STU, JACK, SCOTT, RUDI, KEN, BRAD

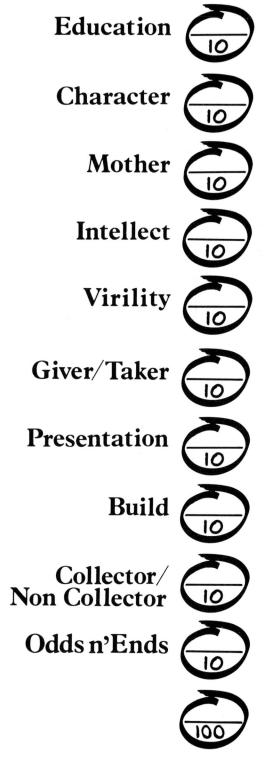

Education /10

Character /10

Mother /10

Intellect /10

Virility /10

Giver/Taker /10

Presentation /10

Build /10

Collector/ Non Collector /10

Odds n'Ends /10

/100

NIGHT PERSON

MIDDLE—UPPER CLASS PARENTS

ALWAYS SEEN SITTING OR LYING DOWN

WEARS MAKE-UP

CLAIMS TO BE BI-SEXUAL

TATTOO ON BODY

BAD BREATH

SMELLS OF JOSS STICKS

HAS MANY FRIENDS OF BOTH SEXES

BADLY BITTEN NAILS

SUFFERS FROM STOMACH PAINS

DRIVES A MINI-MOKE OR JEEP

SMOKES GRASS

(FUN FAGS)

READS KAFKA & N.M.E

In later life . . .

Becomes amazingly respectable – a complete metamorphosis – quite unrecognizable. Stock broker, sings in local choir and plays Beethoven. Quite pleasant, in fact.

Could be . . .

SEBASTIAN, SETH, LANCE, CLINT, ORLANDO, CARY, GARETH

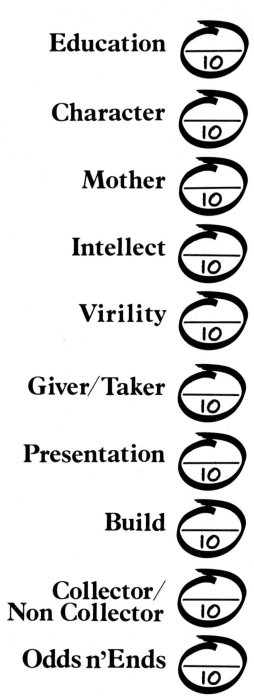

Education 10

Character 10

Mother 10

Intellect 10

Virility 10

Giver/Taker 10

Presentation 10

Build 10

Collector/Non Collector 10

Odds n'Ends 10

100

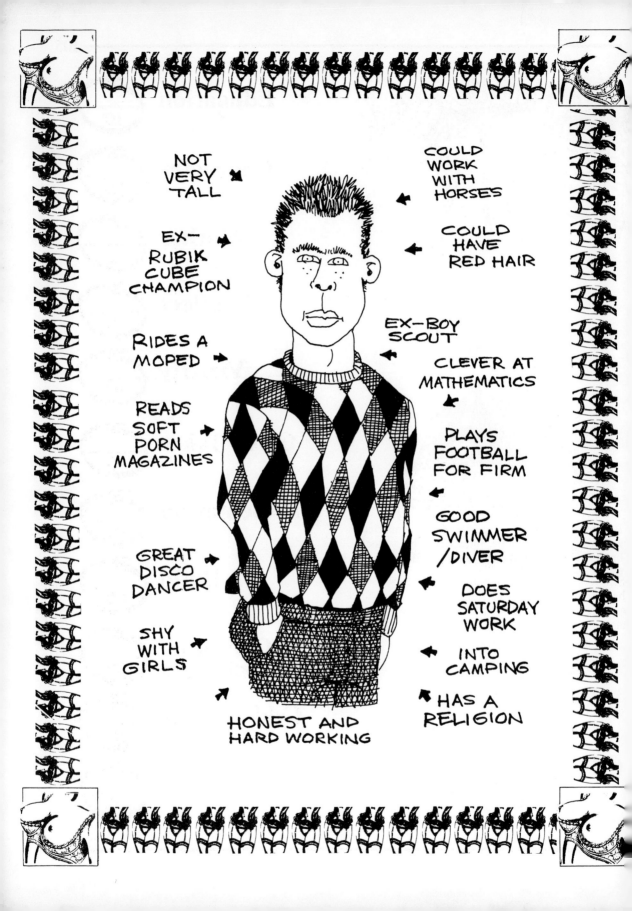

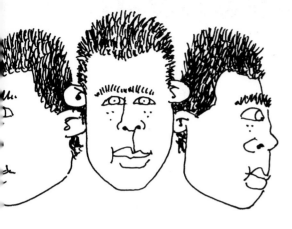

In later life . . .

Still celibate. Has either gone into the Church, or has become rather eccentric. Full of Vision and always into some Mission or another. Into life after death, yoga and faith-healing.

Could be . . .

KERRY, RICKY, IAIN, EDDY, CHRIS, MALCOLM

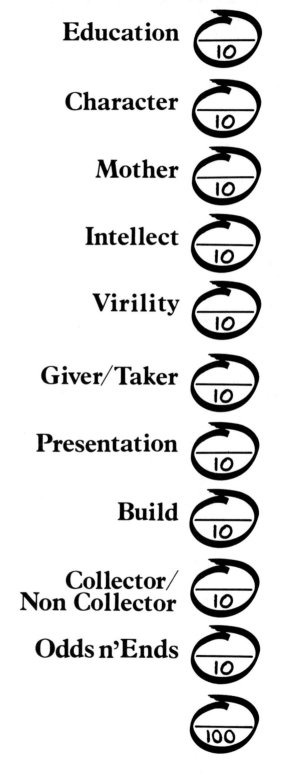

Education — 10

Character — 10

Mother — 10

Intellect — 10

Virility — 10

Giver/Taker — 10

Presentation — 10

Build — 10

Collector/Non Collector — 10

Odds n' Ends — 10

— 100

UNDER THE INFLUENCE

I f you want to avoid anything ranging from deep embarrassment to actual physical assault, you must give serious thought to the effect of alcohol on your man. It can turn the sweetest, suavest, most considerate and charming man into an absolute and utter * * * *. Equally, you must observe just how much he can take before he starts going really squiffy - capacity to take drink varies enormously, and isn't necessarily related to size.

But remember, alcohol is a depressant. The sort of nature that predominates as a regular feature of your man-inebriate could well be his true nature that may on other occasions be carefully held in check. Equally, try and observe his drinking patterns. There are those who choose to drink when the mood and occasion suits; and there are those who actually *need* to drink, may well be secretive drinkers, and will spend a large part of their time in a semi-comatose and accordingly semi-functional state.

The romantic drunk

Gets increasingly affectionate and demanding, and tends to find women - all women - more and more attractive. Drink seldom becomes a debilitating factor and will keep going all night. Fine, if you've got the stamina. Watch for them lurking in dark corners for unsuspecting ladies at parties. Tend to lose most sense of discrimination.

The benign drunk

Just sits and smiles beamishly. Seldom offensive. Will leave you to wash up. Probably rather ineffectual generally, but likes to feel liked. Not too bright - a bit of a plodder. To be found curled up in some dark corner or swaying gently in the corridor after the party has finished.

The angry drunk

This one really can be dangerous. Personality changes completely and can become not just angry, but terrifyingly violent. Could thump you - hard. Becomes highly irrational. Extreme examples can rape and even murder. Certainly smash your home up.

The lonely drinker

Basically shy and insecure - or just plain ugly. Will drink to drown his reservations and fear of rejection, and to help him pluck up the courage he so miserably lacks. By the time he's ready to approach you - he'll be too smashed anyway.

The jolly drunk

Can be great fun if you're in the mood. Everything and everyone becomes vastly entertaining. Gets into his joke routine eventually - and expects you to find it as funny as he, and stick it out to the end. Usually winds up making something of a fool of himself - and possibly you as well.

UNDER THE INFLUENCE

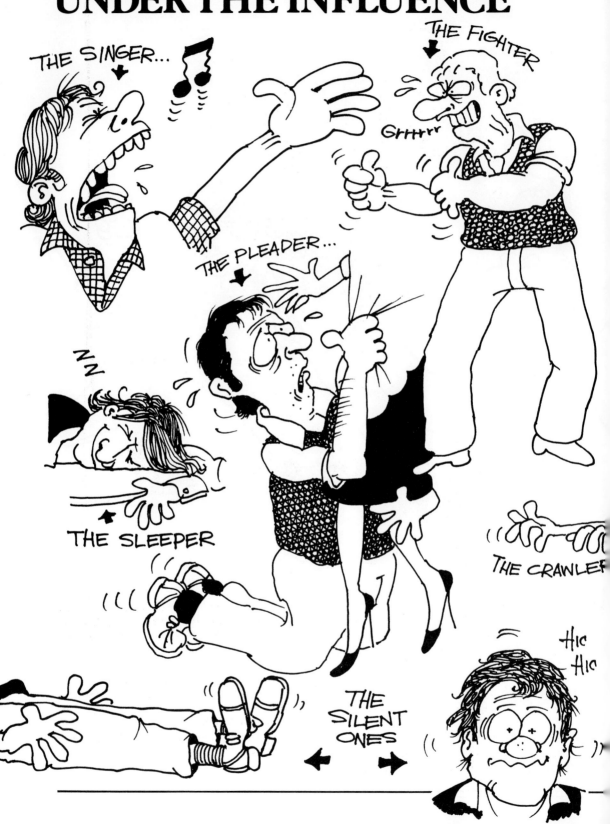

THE LOVER

The voluble drunk

Especially to be found in the company of other, like, men. Gets louder and louder to overcome basic insecurity. Gestures get wilder, achievements in life more extravagant. The true, raw Hooray Henry type or would-be Trade Union leader. On the whole, objectionable. Regular drinkers and complainers. Make dire tourists.

The team-leader drinker

Actually rather a pretender. Will drink wine and soda, and fix doubles for everyone else. Loves to be and appear to be in control, so hates to get drunk - but needs to get his troops drunk in order to assume that control. Pretty miserable, really.

The ceremonial working-class drinker

Desperate, often angry, feeling of inferiority gives him a driving need to impress - somehow. Often the only way he can impress (or thinks he can) is by drinking everyone else under the table. Unfortunate.

DRINKING HABITS

GULPERS

The home-boozer

Doesn't really like to go out boozing with the lads - or even let people know about his drinking. Seems antisocial, even dull. Actually rather sad. Doesn't have much faith in himself - and doesn't much trust others either. Feels safest in his own, protected, alcohol-dimmed cocoon.

The aggressive drunk

Watch out here. Maybe putting on a big show to cover up the fact that he's too drunk to Make It. Hates to think others are more capable, so very generous with the rounds. Fundamentally highly insecure, and probably aware of it. Can be vicious; usually life's failures. You may be in to masochism.

The addicted drunk

Sad cases, these. Any excuse to drink. Watch out for Dettol bottles full of Gin. Become very accomplished deceivers, and besotted with drink and where the next one is coming from. Big red noses and shaky hands are common. Won't eat, and lose interest in appearance and cleanliness. Make sure his will is properly sewn up.

SUCKERS

SWIGGERS

SIPPERS

SNIFFERS

The melancholic drinker

Life is Just Too Bad. Will wind up crying - to be seen with head in plate and gravy dripping down his tie. Don't be suprised if no-one takes any notice - probably does it every night. Could be titled.

The fast drinker

Totally messed up. Seeking oblivion by getting smashed as fast as possible. Could be a short-term phase. More serious cases will be found in a couple of years' time under the arches surrounded by Meths bottles.

WAVERS
(CHEERS)

LOOKERS

The tippler

Genuinely enjoys the sensation of being slightly tiddly nearly all the time. Always topping up his unwashed glass from the last drink. Bottles all over the place - usually half-full. In the pub at opening time or a frequenter of afternoon wine-bars. Not dangerous - just plain dull.

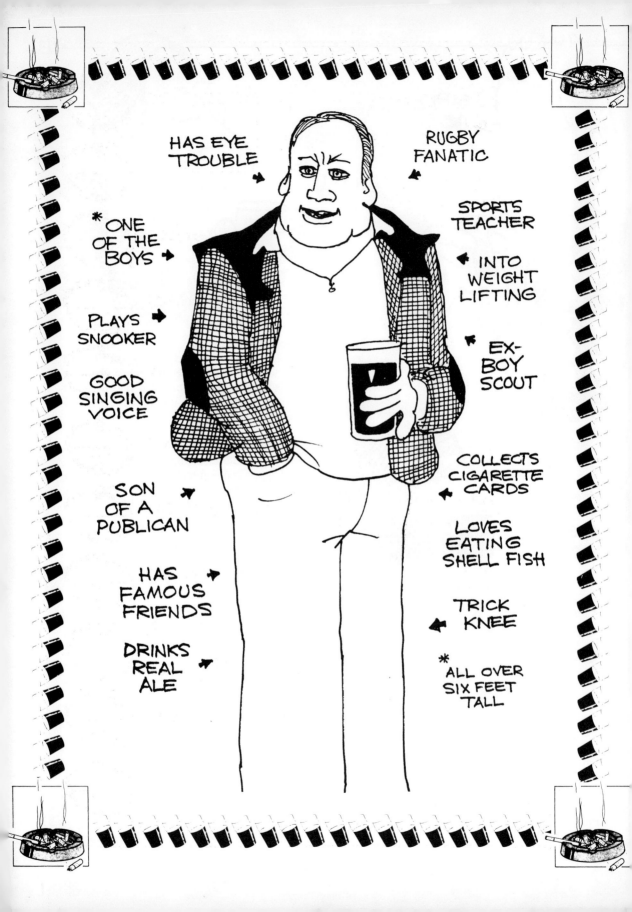

In later life . . .

Has probably made a pile, but doesn't like to show it. Runs 2 Rolls Royce cars and a battery chicken farm. Is well into his third marriage. Still enjoys a beer at the local.

Could be . . .

TERRY, CHIC, JOCK, NOSHER, BOB, STAN

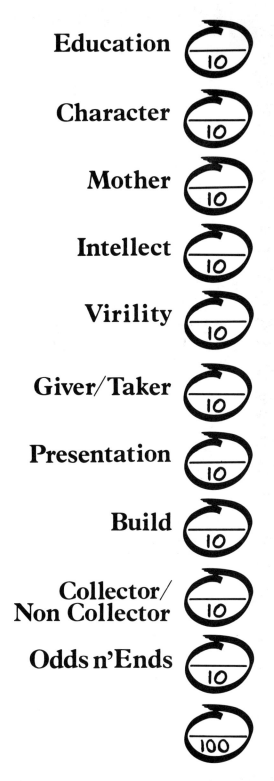

Education — 10

Character — 10

Mother — 10

Intellect — 10

Virility — 10

Giver/Taker — 10

Presentation — 10

Build — 10

Collector/Non Collector — 10

Odds n'Ends — 10

— 100

 Education 10

 Character 10

 Mother 10

 Intellect 10

 Virility 10

 Giver/Taker 10

 Presentation 10

 Build 10

 Collector/ Non Collector 10

 Odds n'Ends 10

 100

In later life . . .

Very hard, cold, callous and calculating. Owns a newspaper or magazine. Runs 2 mistresses and a boyfriend. Good supply of leather straps in the bedroom. A nasty piece of work. Supremely lazy.

Could be . . .

JEREMY, RODDIE, MAX, JAMES, MARCUS, JULIAN

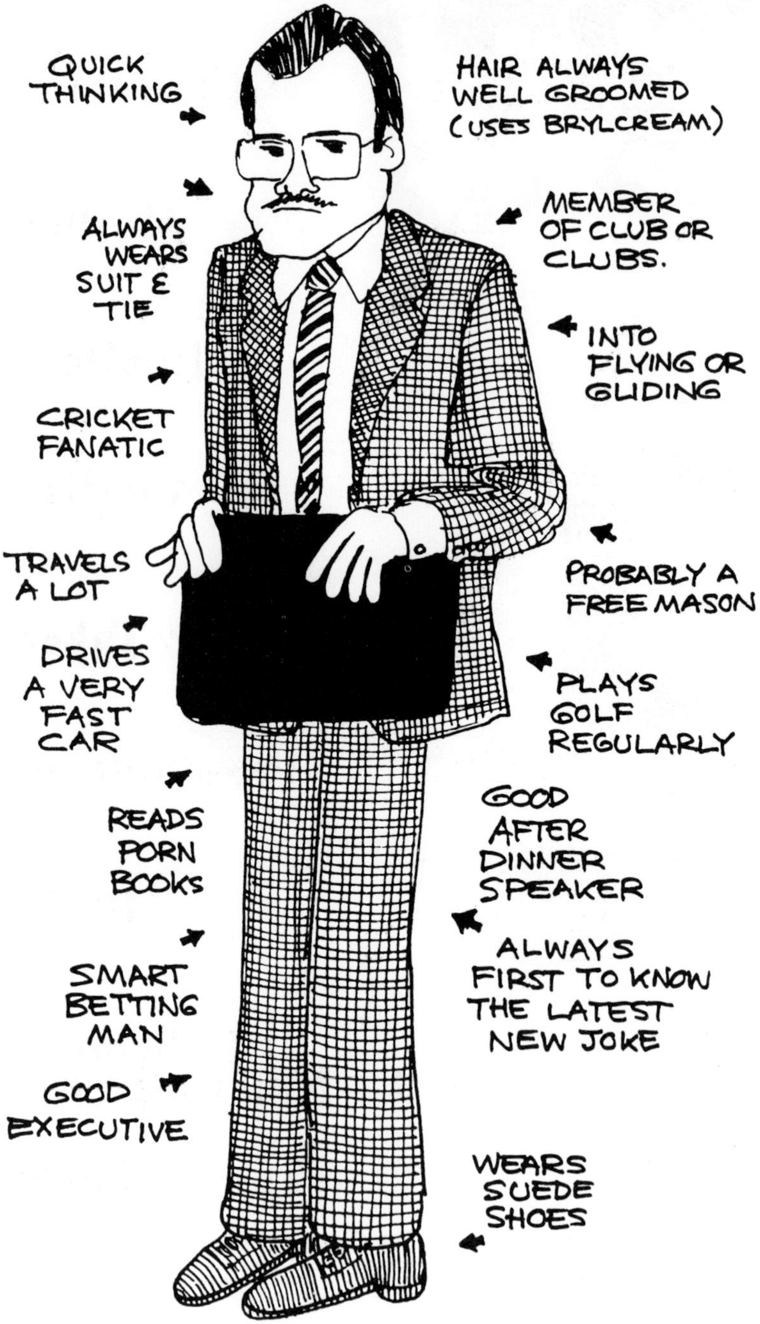

QUICK THINKING

HAIR ALWAYS WELL GROOMED (USES BRYLCREAM)

ALWAYS WEARS SUIT & TIE

MEMBER OF CLUB OR CLUBS.

INTO FLYING OR GLIDING

CRICKET FANATIC

TRAVELS A LOT

PROBABLY A FREE MASON

DRIVES A VERY FAST CAR

PLAYS GOLF REGULARLY

READS PORN BOOKS

GOOD AFTER DINNER SPEAKER

SMART BETTING MAN

ALWAYS FIRST TO KNOW THE LATEST NEW JOKE

GOOD EXECUTIVE

WEARS SUEDE SHOES

In later life . . .

Never married. Has millionaire girlfriends all round the world. Probably in the media business. Has private pilot's licence and drinks rye whisky. Member of the Reform Club and the Royal Geographical Society.

Could be . . .

ALAN, WILLIAM, LESLIE, LEWIS, DENNIS, CUTHBERT, VICTOR, TREVOR

Education   10

Character   10

Mother   10

Intellect   10

Virility   10

Giver/Taker   10

Presentation   10

Build   10

Collector/Non Collector   10

Odds n' Ends   10

100

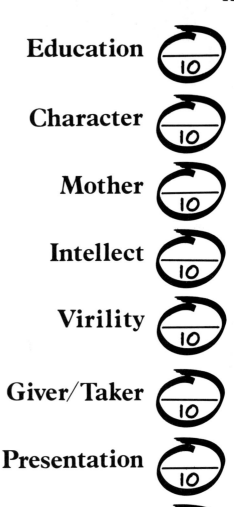

THE SINGLE MAN

Check out his habitat if you can - it will tell you a great deal about him.

Thoroughly chaotic:

Ranges from fun mess to total squalor. Most who live in fun mess are both revelling in freedom and the rejection of the orderly maternal home environment - and looking for someone to look after him. Extreme cases will be terrified of relationships; enough squalor to put you off. Equally, any such relationship just *has* to be better, and the mess-hovel is created as a prop to help that relationship get off to an advantaged start. Generally, the untidier a man is, the easier he is to catch - but some things should be watched for as signs to Avoid Like the Plague: pictures of naked men on walls - or teddy-bears in bed; blow-up women hidden beneath underwear; endless half-empty cans of food sprouting six months' mould; items of make-up and ladies' clothing.

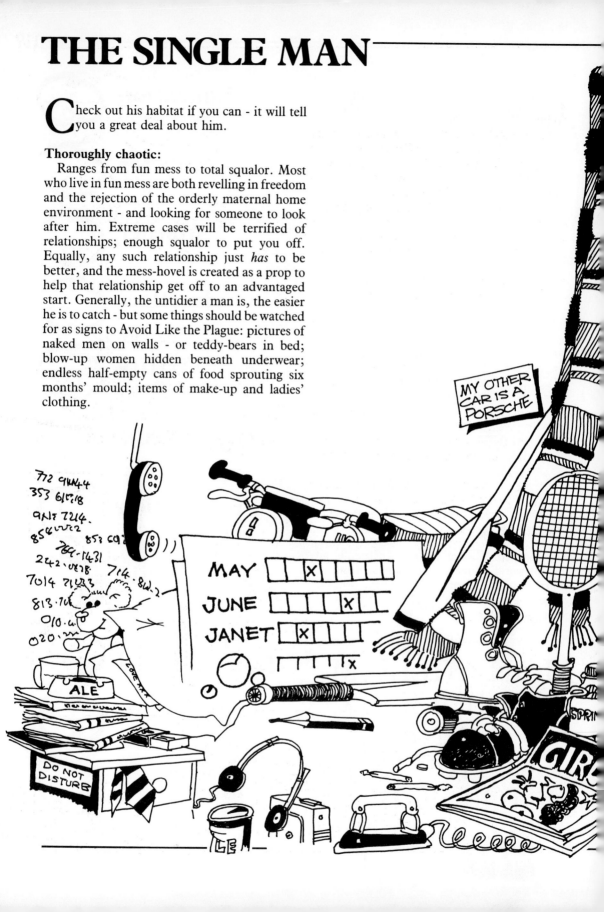

Tidy:

The clinically orderly - home like a hospital, not a speck of dust in sight? Careful; you may be in the den of an a-sexual. Just generally orderly - and you've hit a trad. conformist with parental support; sports car, silver candlesticks, a tea set, formal dinner parties. Takes washing home to Mummy every week-end - very much looking for a Mum-substitute and will marry Correctly to please parents and ensure inheritance. Not a strong man. The deceptively orderly - rolls of clothes stuffed into drawers, open tins of baked beans under the bed? Good - he's promising.

The single man is recognisable out of habitat - often wears strong after-shave to counteract the Single-Man's-Smell - that strange combination of bacon fat, must, stale sweat, fish-and-chips and just plain dirt. Clothes often crumpled or dirty - sweat marks on shirt armpits, hates ironing. Lingers in launderettes; talks compulsively about Exploits With Women; collects things - the Single Man's Trophies - pub beer mugs, road signs, girl's underwear, empty wine bottles etc.

Whether he's actively out looking for a mate, or playing the field until Miss Right comes along, he's likely to be a little afraid still of women. If you're looking for a permanent partnership, it's obviously an area with which you must familiarise yourself.

CHAT-UP LINES

USES
HAIR DYE →

BORN
MIDDLE
AGED →

HAS
GREAT EYE →
FOR CUTTING
PRIVET
HEDGES

HAS
← AGED
MOTHER

ON
LOCAL →
COUNCIL

BELONGS
TO THE
MAGIC
CIRCLE
←

COULD
BE A →
CHURCH
WARDEN

WATCHES
THE VAL
DOONICAN
SHOW
←

MEMBER
OF LOCAL
AMATEUR
DRAMATIC
SOCIETY →

CARRIES
MONEY IN
LEATHER
PURSE
←

OWNS →
BOTH HOVER
& QUALCAST
MOWER

MAKES
HIS OWN
WINE
←

ONCE MET
BING
CROSBY
→

PLAYS
GOLF
←

Education 10

Character 10

Mother 10

Intellect 10

Virility 10

Giver/Taker 10

Presentation 10

Build 10

Collector/Non Collector 10

Odds n'Ends 10

 100

In later life . . .

The same – for ever – and ever – and ever.

Could be . . .

HERBERT, HORACE, GEORGE, HAROLD, WILLIAM

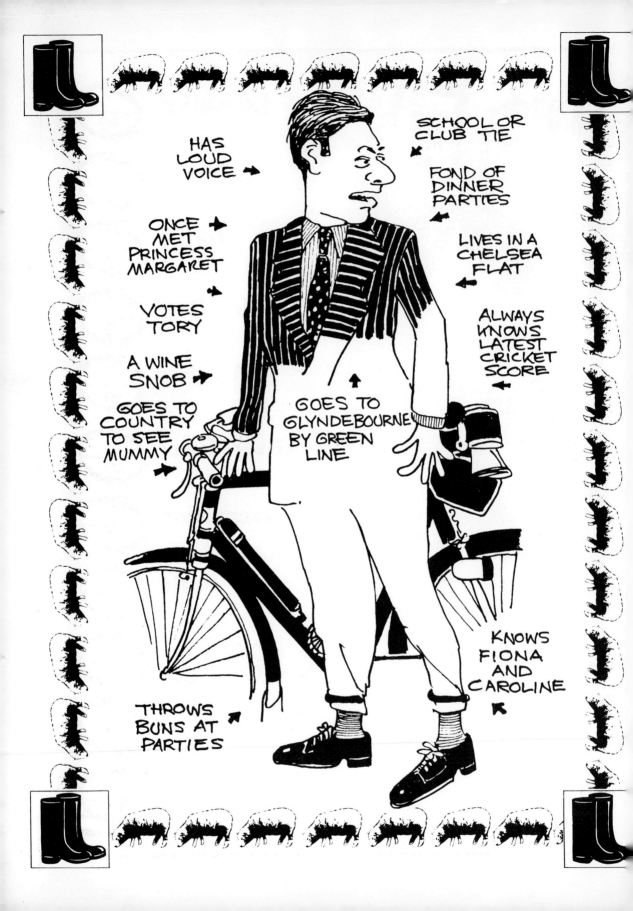

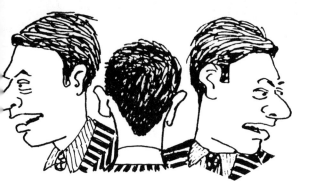

In later life . . .

Establishment figure. On the way to a Knighthood for achieving precisely nothing – but has kept in with all the Right People.

Could be . . .

HENRY, EDGAR, CHARLES, NIGEL, JEREMY, RODERICK

Education

Character

Mother

Intellect

Virility

Giver/Taker

Presentation

Build

Collector/ Non Collector

Odds n'Ends

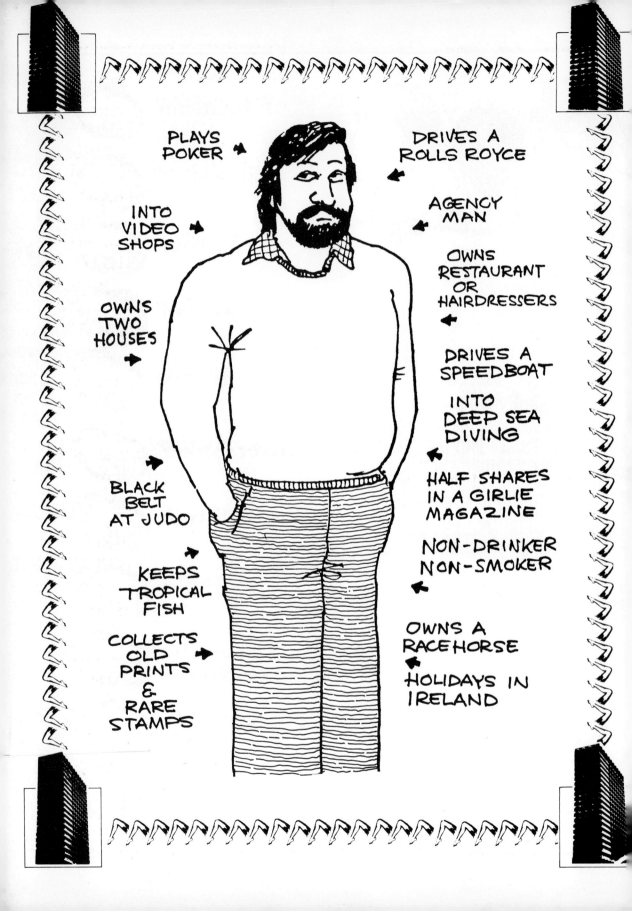

In later life . . .

Has had three bankruptcies, 3 Rolls Royces, 4 wives, and 2 strokes. Still at it. Probably has a house in the Caribbean and a resident medical staff.

Could be . . .

MARTIN, MATTHEW, STUART, PATRICK, REG, GAVIN, ROY

Education

Character

Mother

Intellect

Virility

Giver/Taker

Presentation

Build

Collector/ Non Collector

Odds n'Ends

SPOT THE MARRIED MAN

A vital talent, and to be fostered with all speed and dedication, and on all counts - whether you're looking for marital bliss, or just want to be a pampered mistress.

There are two basic sorts of married men; those are aren't happily married, and are genuinely looking for a Nice Girl; and those who are perfectly happy with their married state, thank-you-very-much, but like variety and a bit of froth.

Most married men will carefully avoid talking about their home environment for as long as possible. Tend to be looking for something absolutely in contrast to their own lives, be it genuine loving happiness, or erotic naughty-knicker fantasy. Most Peacocks and Groupies will wear some sort of wedding ring, if not on the appropriate finger. Chameleons are harder to suss out. Note the following signs:

The partially-clothed syndrome

Also the sequential-undresser - outer clothes near the door, socks and underpants by the bed. Ready for a fast get-away. Probably avid, passionate and quick to get to the point, but may not complete the job satisfactorily. Sudden noises send him flying out of bed. Traffic drawing to a halt outside and headlights lead to car-tus interruptus. Tends to run fingers through hair. Again, probably basically faithful.

The carrier-bag syndrome

Last-minute decision, fast-worker. Rushes out to buy clean shirt and underwear. Very nervous - clutches his carrier bag, twitches, and drives fast. Not basically unfaithful. Doubtful if he'll make it on the first or even third time.

The Clock-Watcher

Not as well organised as he would like to be. Sets his wrist watch alarm, and manipulates you so that he can see the dial over your shoulder. Probably an unsatisfactory lover as a result. Keeps ringing the Talking Clock - Just To Make Sure. Try and get him away for a long week-end to test out his real colours. Probably not basically unfaithful either, but not too happily married.

The Eccentric

Will probably confuse you totally, until you've sussed out what it's all about. Takes you to bizarre, way-out restaurants where none of his friends would ever go - and nor would you, for that matter. Talks very quietly and intensely. Likes subdued, almost non-existent lighting, and will want to make love in the dark, with heavy music on the stereo. Again, probably determinedly married.

The Domestic

Settles in and makes himself at home. Feeds the cats and washes up. Enjoys doing nothing with you, and will happily spend an evening eating fish and chips in front of the television. Deeply affectionate and highly tactile. Probably very pleased to be with you, and is genuinely unhappily married to some dreadful dragon.

The Stud

Determinedly married, mistress-collector. Very smooth and practised in the art of infidelity. Will give you flowers and chocolates, but never scent - unless it's the same as his wife uses - and prefers you without make-up. Knows how to keep his clothes looking immaculate, and arranges everything, including week-ends away, very neatly and tidily. Has an inexhaustible supply of inventive excuses which will doubtless be used on you when he finds his next mistress. Beware The Stud.

EXCUSES

In later life . . .

Running local film society and cricket club. Plays bowls. House full of cosy collections. Enjoys gardening. Kindly and sociable, but basically useless.

Could be . . .

MATTHEW, CORIN, COLIN, HEDLEY, PETER, ARTHUR, ANTHONY

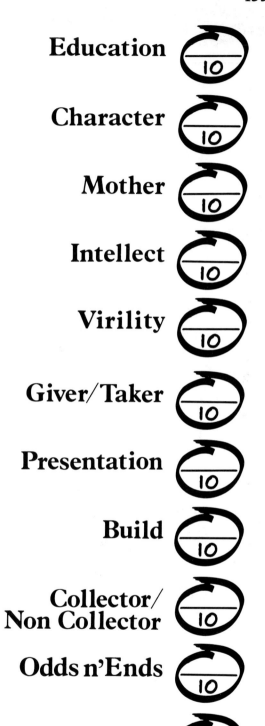

Education — 10

Character — 10

Mother — 10

Intellect — 10

Virility — 10

Giver/Taker — 10

Presentation — 10

Build — 10

Collector/Non Collector — 10

Odds n'Ends — 10

— 100

In later life . . .

Still dreaming. Might have struck it rich. Still trying to stay young and trendy. Probably quiet and prone to be moody.

Could be . . .

BRIAN, BILL, PAUL, LARRY, STANLEY, SIDNEY

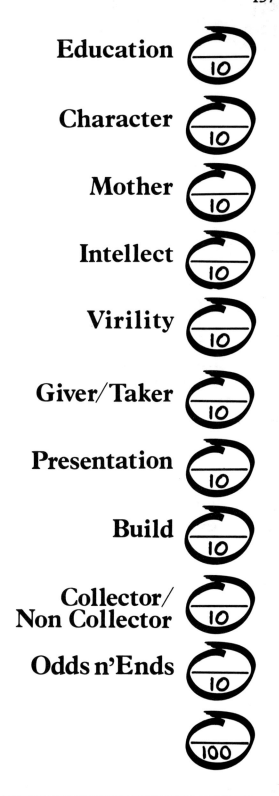

Education 10

Character 10

Mother 10

Intellect 10

Virility 10

Giver/Taker 10

Presentation 10

Build 10

Collector/ Non Collector 10

Odds n'Ends 10

100

In later life . . .

Biggles flies again.

Could be . . .

ANDREW, ANDY, ANDRE, RANDY, DANDY, SANDY & Co

Education 10

Character 10

Mother 10

Intellect 10

Virility 10

Giver/Taker 10

Presentation 10

Build 10

Collector/ Non Collector 10

Odds n'Ends 10

 100

SEXUAL FANTASIES

A ll men have fantasies – some quite simple and straight-forward, and some bordering on the bizarre. Most men keep their fantasies to themselves, and will be satisfied by reading naughty magazines, gossip in men's clubs, and the odd blue movie.

If you come across his short trousers and school cap in his brief case – start worrying. Otherwise, most fantasies are quite harmless and VERY IMPORTANT – if his fantasies are, to you, tolerable – some could even be fun – do try and join in. He'll appreciate it enormously, and it will deepen and strengthen your relationship – quite apart from spicing it up. Don't drive him to another theatre – let him fantasize you on *your* stage.

There are the totally suppressed fantasizers: not much to say about them, as you'll never find out what their fantasies are, if they allow themselves to have them at all. A shame, really.

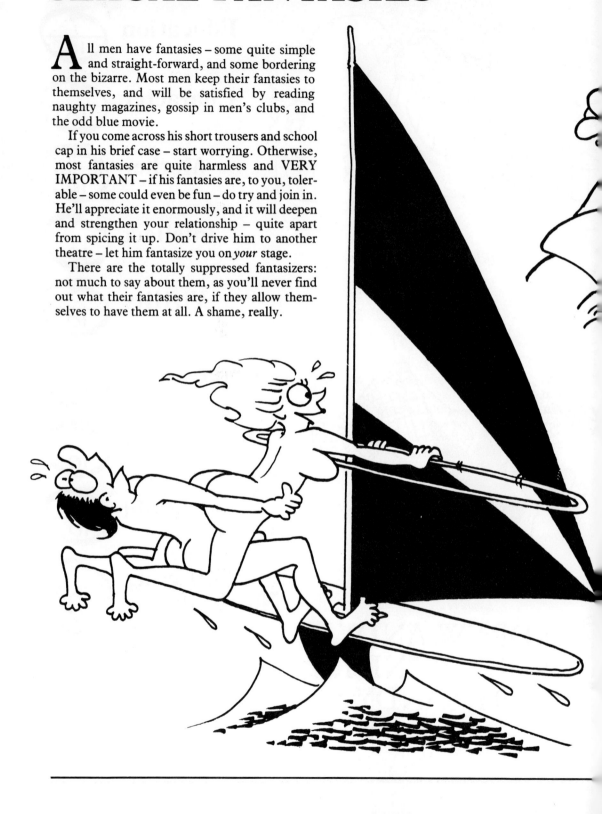

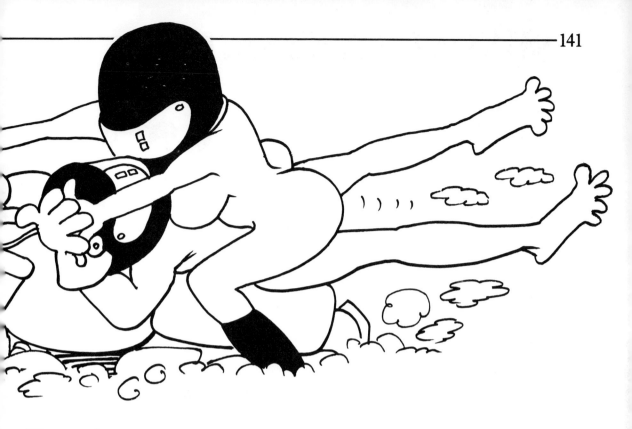

Those on the cusp: quite easy to spot; love fancy-dress parties; tend to stop for nubile hitch-hikers; have pin-up calendars and a healthy sprinkling of naughty magazines. Try putting on your gym slip and long socks, tie your hair in bunches and see how he reacts. Could be fun.

SEXUAL FANTASIES

The practitioners: you may need to be wary of these, depending on the sort of person you are. Will organise wife-swappings with gusto, buy you kinky underwear, pinch ladies' bottoms, and seduce his secretary. Reliability is not his middle name. Worthy of serious reservations unless you go in for the same games.

The bizarre: The 40,000 Leagues Under the Sea and Above the Grounders. Watch out – likely to drag you into the cloakroom on the inter-city. Could be the masked raider in that last porno movie you saw. Spotting *HIM* involves a considerable depth of anatomical knowledge.

PUDDING BASIN HAIRCUT

POOR EYESIGHT

THICK GLASSES

UNDER FIVE FEET SIX IN HEIGHT

HAND KNITTED SWEATER

FOND OF PARKS AND OPEN SPACES

SOILED RAINCOAT EXTRA LARGE FITTING

LEAVES IN HIS HAIR FROM HIDING IN BUSHES

SWEETS IN POCKET

FLIES UNDONE

BAGGY SUIT TROUSERS

(TURN-UPS)

VERY SMALL FEET

LACED SHOES

Education

Character

Mother

Intellect

In later life . . .

Long since put away out of harm's way. Still optimistic – always hanging around in dark passages.

Virility

Giver/Taker

Presentation

Build

Collector/ Non Collector

Odds n'Ends

Could be . . .

LUKE, SID, KENNETH, OLIVER, LESTER, LEONARD

SEXUAL VARIATIONS & DEVIATIONS

Something is definitely unhinged here - either mentally or hormonally. Not much point in trying to change them - just try and understand, and then accept it or get out while the going's good. If he needs to break eggs on your breasts before making love, so be it. Buy dozens and dozens of eggs. If proclivities border on the (to you) insane, then run, and chalk it up to experience.

The effeminate male:

Dresses up (probably transexual) - the gay who doesn't really realise it. Tries to form relationships with women and *be* a woman. Hyper fastidiousness and preening in front of mirrors are the norm. If he realises he's really homosexual, you're likely to come home and find your husband in bed with another man. Very sad.

The male Gay:

Even more masculine than men. Can be difficult to spot. Very macho: always increasing his biceps.

The female Gay:

Obvious; make smashing friends; play the female role to the male Gay; kindly, homely, considerate and excellent listeners. Never threatening.

The Sadist:

Ones who want to inflict pain, and watch its effect. Tend to wear leathers and big boots - thoroughly studded up. Fundamentally deeply insecure in their own masculinity, and need to cause brutality to reassure themselves. Thoroughly nasty.

GLITTER

The Masochist:

Terribly sad, these. The self-imposed scapegoats in life. Please hurt me and blame me. Go around looking like hang-dog Whippets. Forever apologizing.

ADVICE: An area to avoid like the plague if you want to live a happily heterosexual life. There are plenty of specialist books around if you are interested.

EXERCISE FREAKS

Men will exercise for a variety of reasons. Some will reckon making love is the best form of exercise ever invented – and if you've got the stamina, great.

Others go in for all sorts of Exercise Exercise – from the occasional swoosh round the swimming pool or game of tennis, through to the demented joggers and the thoroughly narcissistic body-builders. Some will do it because they know a certain amount of exercise is *good* for them – others because they think it enhances their macho image. Middle age is a time to watch – that creeping paunch, suspicious wobble under the chin, preference for taking lifts rather than climbing stairs. On go the sneakers, and off they puff. Probably do themselves a world of good – within reason.

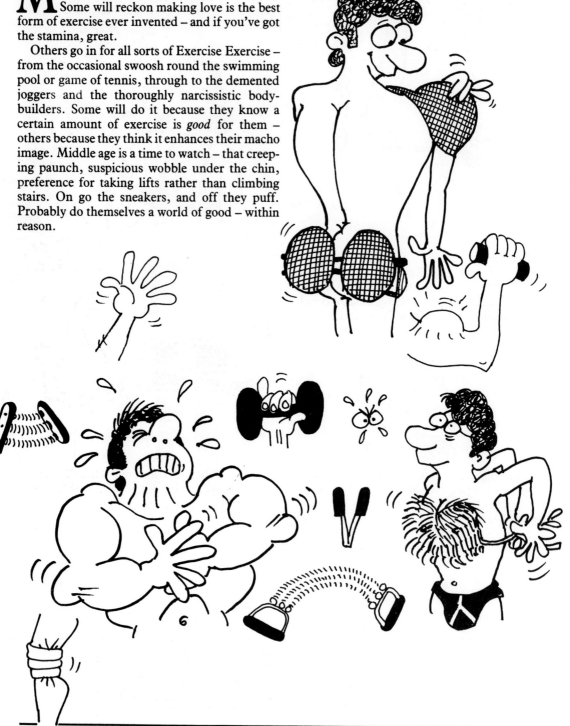

Oh, but the extremes, the dedicated demons of the work-out gym, the daily leapers on to the bathroom scales, the pummelers of sub-epidermal fat globules. You've got an obsessive case on your hands. With any luck, he'll be carried off with a fearsome heart attack before he's managed to bore *you* to death. Or he'll join the primeval group screaming sessions – which will at least give you some peace.

THE EMOTIONAL MAN

To most men, the demonstration of emotions is a very Non-Masculine thing to do. Which is pretty silly, really, since to deny emotions is to deny humanity, and the occasional healthy release never does any harm.

As a reaction to all this suppression, men who do show their emotions do it in an almost explosive way. And there are those who simply are naturally hyper-emotional – probably even more so than women.

The Terrified Timmies:
Life is one long journey of dread and fear. Everything is complicated and hostile. Everything Must Go Wrong. For them, it usually does. Probably into masochism.

The Weepies:
Basically, can't cope with emotions at all. Tear ducts constantly un-plugged. Likely to read women's romances and bawl their eyes out at the soppy bits. Doubtful if they could get the words out through the tears – if they ever pluck up the courage – to propose. Watch out for a huge consumption of paper hankies.

The Vicious Victors:

Extremely unpleasant, these – if not plain dangerous. Rant and rave and scream invective abuse at the most minor upset. Smash up the house and hurl cats out of windows. Expensive and even physically painful. With luck, will die of a peptic ulcer at an early age.

The Scaredy-cats:

Just plain failures. Never pluck up the courage to do anything. Frightened of the dark, spiders and People. Need total Hot House protection. Wets the bed.

The Romantic:

Rather sad, if touching. Gentle people, but utterly dependent on a dedicated female partner. Can't cope without her. Follow you around the house like a puppy. Go quite bananas over romantic mementos and anniversaries. Highly claustrophobic.

EATING HABITS

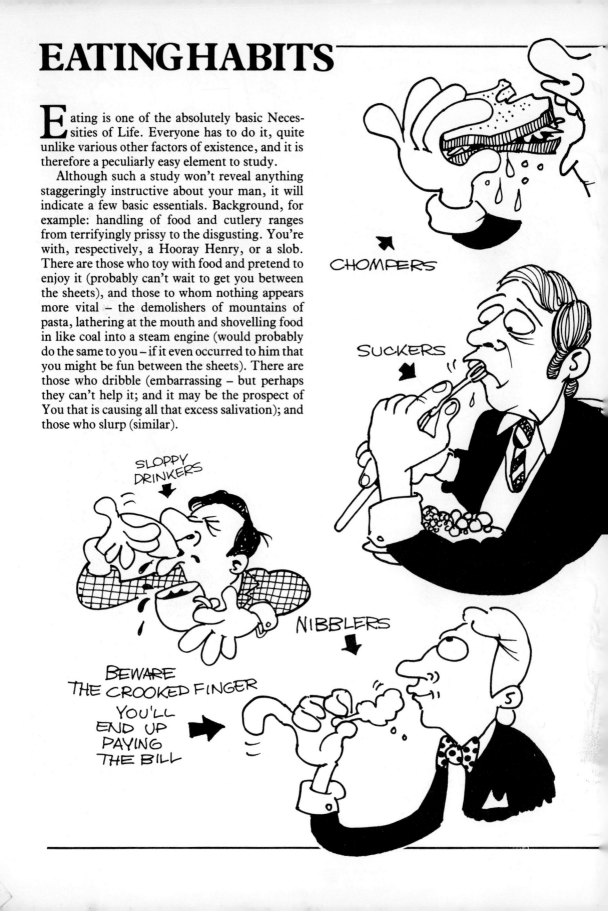

Eating is one of the absolutely basic Necessities of Life. Everyone has to do it, quite unlike various other factors of existence, and it is therefore a peculiarly easy element to study.

Although such a study won't reveal anything staggeringly instructive about your man, it will indicate a few basic essentials. Background, for example: handling of food and cutlery ranges from terrifyingly prissy to the disgusting. You're with, respectively, a Hooray Henry, or a slob. There are those who toy with food and pretend to enjoy it (probably can't wait to get you between the sheets), and those to whom nothing appears more vital – the demolishers of mountains of pasta, lathering at the mouth and shovelling food in like coal into a steam engine (would probably do the same to you – if it even occurred to him that you might be fun between the sheets). There are those who dribble (embarrassing – but perhaps they can't help it; and it may be the prospect of You that is causing all that excess salivation); and those who slurp (similar).

CHOMPERS

SUCKERS

SLOPPY DRINKERS

NIBBLERS

BEWARE THE CROOKED FINGER YOU'LL END UP PAYING THE BILL

There are those who tackle food with an intense dedication to its excellence or otherwise (liable to be pedantic – possibly a stock broker or bank manager); and those who treat it with a total lack of interest (which could well extend to you, too – Just Another Meal, syndrome).

And there are those who enjoy food, appreciate it, eat it with dignity but relish, and treat good food as the true gift it is. He'll probably treat you the same way.

FOREIGNERS

Here's a whole new ball game. Away from their usual environment, the tendency to outrageous extremes is the norm. Do all the naughty things they wouldn't dare do back home. Likely to propose instantly – and then vanish.

Could be enlivening for a quick fling – but *don't fall in love.* Or pick a sheik.

TURKISH EGYPTIAN OR STREET ENTERTAINER

GERMAN OR AUSTRIAN

AMERICAN OR CHINESE

LOONY

FRENCH OR CANADIAN

COULD BE BRITISH

IRISH OR IRISH AMER

COULD BE A SPY – OR RUSSIAN

ITALIAN CYPRIOT OR ALGERIAN

PROBABLY DUTCH

So what's the score?

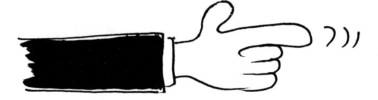

THE ULTIMATE SCORES

There are two vital factors in intelligent and revealing man-spotting: accurate perception and interpretation of the fundamental elements; and accurate rating, or scoring, of those interpretations.

If you have assiduously studied this book and followed its exhortations, you will have been scoring the representative characters that have appeared. These two pages reveal to you the real scores that have been diligently provided for you by The Experts. If your final scores are within 5 points of those given on these pages, you are well on course to becoming an extremely proficient Spotter. If you are more than 10 points out, it would be beneficial to look again at the characters and analyse them rather more carefully – but you're on the right track. If you are 15 or more points out, well, you're really rather way off beam. Start again with the Fundamentals. It's worth it. For your sake – if not for his.

YOUR D.I.Y. CHECKLIST

On the opposite page appears a void Person, and a void set of scores. This is provided for your convenience, to complete as you deem appropriate in relation to your own man. It is recommended that this section is treated with caution, and that soft pencil is used to complete it. For it may be that, having learnt the correct rudiments of scoring and applied it to Him (and don't do so until you have rated well on the pre-scored charts of the characters in this book), you may find that he is decidedly sub-standard. In which case, you can rub him out (both figuratively and literally) – and Start Again.

Here is a Check List for you to consult when you're finally in a position to score Your Man:

Hair:
Is it real? (check your insurance before you tug too hard – those knitted ones cost a fortune); long and dirty (drugs?); scratching (probably has nits and five kids); short (IBM, army or metamorphosing punk); long blond (Nordic or transexual); black (could be Celtic); ginger – and on knees (probably Scottish); Blue rinse(!)

Shoes:
Polished or unpolished? military? boots; spurs; sporty; slippers; wellingtons, suede, etc.

Jacket:
Country check; suit; dandruff shoulders; worn elbows; frayed cuffs; odd; studded; bomber, etc.

Trousers:
Baggy; tight; very tight (Italian?); short; very short (American?) gun in pocket? threadbare; home-knitted; silk; leather; cod piece; velcro flies; dungarees; breeches, etc.

Shirt:
Frills; striped; unattached collar; dog-collar; no collar; flowery; frayed cuffs; frayed collar; reversed collar (Mum loves him); silk; hair shirt; T-shirt.

Tie:
Stripe; old school or club; brigade (fire or army); bow; knitted; string; leather; clip-on; cravat, etc.

Hat:
To hide bald patch? skull cap; plastic rainbood; beret (French?); Texan; Tyrolean; knotted handkerchief (could be English); deer stalker; bowler; police helmet, etc.

Underpants:
Floppy with holes; very tight (careful); string; jock strap; boxers; thermal; disposable; none (watch it); dirty (check his medical record); M & S (much practised); rude message (impotent) etc.

Vest:
If in Summer, probably married; string; stained armpits (poor); sporty; rude message; Freudian slips (probably Gay); thermal with long sleeves (yachtsman or nutter) etc.

Socks:
Odd; long; garters; wrinkled; holes; well-darned (married), etc.

Trappings:
Masses of jewellery (careful); combs and pens in pocket; belt (conscious of waist); braces; gold medallion (rich – or wants you to think he is); camera; clutch bag (careful); spotted silk hankie; brief-case with overnight clothes compartment; etc.

Otherwise, just keep a weather-eye open for twitches, scratching, mannerisms and gesticulations, etc.; an ear open for speech accents, impediments; grunts, etc.; and a nose open for offensive or prissy smells.

Get scoring!

The Manalysis Chart

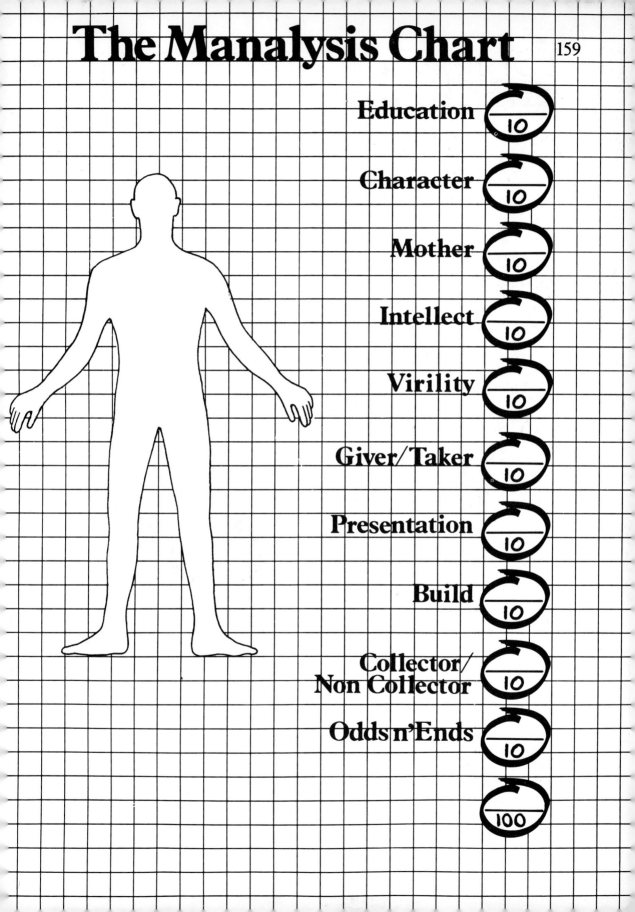

Education /10

Character /10

Mother /10

Intellect /10

Virility /10

Giver/Taker /10

Presentation /10

Build /10

Collector/ Non Collector /10

Odds n'Ends /10

/100

"DARLING, THERE WAS THIS RATHER DRUNKEN
TATTOOIST AT MY STAG PARTY LAST NIGHT..."